How come...?
Why this very German perspective on Writing and Democracy translated into English?

Have you forgotten already where the mindset of modern democracy, individual freedoms, and rational thought was lifted up to our societies? It was during the Enlightenment, a time when thinkers dared to question authority, challenge tradition, and imagine a world where reasoning became our shared responsibility. This is our legacy: the art of human feedback.

In history, we tend to oversimplify the reputation of a nation, attributing its character to so-called *great men*, while overlooking the countless individuals whose voices collectively shape its path. Democracy, as this book shows, thrives not on the proclamations of the few, but on the contributions of the many.

This vital read reminds us that every word we write already reflects the shape of our thoughts, and every thought carries the seeds of our actions. This is not a book about not writing, far from it. It's a book that dares to ask: how can we write, think, and speak in ways that foster connection rather than division?
With humor, reflection, and sharp insight, this work invites us to see language not as a neutral tool, but as the essence of democracy itself. For in the end, democracy is not forged by the heroes alone, but by the stories we tell together. And every story begins with the careful crafting of a single word.
So, let us write, not for greatness, but for understanding, and in doing so, contribute with our human feedback to the narratives that built our democracies.

No
Book
WRITING

... For MORE Democracy!

Translation of   "Kein Buch SCHREIBEN   ... zu MEHR Demokratie!"

Cologne © 2024   *Vera Ansén*

Bibliografische Information der Deutschen Nationalbibliothek: Die Deutsche Nationalbibliothek verzeichnet diese Publikation in der Deutschen Nationalbibliografie; detaillierte bibliografische Daten sind im Internet über dnb.dnb.de abrufbar.

Erstauflage
© 2025 *Vera Ansén*

Idee, Text & Grafik: Vera Ansén
Lektorat: Rebecca Ansén, Köln
Verlag: BoD · Books on Demand GmbH, In de Tarpen 42, 22848 Norderstedt, bod@bod.de
Druck: Libri Plureos GmbH, Friedensallee 273, 22763 Hamburg

ISBN: 978-3-7693-1573-8

Table of Contents

OFFICER (OFF)
(cutting tone)
See this piece of evidence? What is it?

AUTHOR
Some thoughts?

OFFICER
(angrily)
Two languages, in print and digital!
Are you claiming
this wasn't you?

AUTHOR
(quietly)
I did it...

OFFICER
(lowering voice)
Do you think we wouldn't notice?
"No Book Writing"? How stupid
do you think we are?

AUTHOR
(with more emphasis)
I confess, I did it.
(softer)
More than once...

OFFICER
(knowingly)
...and you're going to do it again

AUTHOR
(silently nods)

I confess, I'm a repeat offender ...   When I was young, I was *certain* that by the time I turned 50, I would be writing books. Deliberately, I set out to gather life experiences, determined never to bore anyone. Of course, boredom isn't as bad as its reputation, but boring books? They waste time, burden the environment, and at best, offer an escape from reality. The fact remains: we use language — for all sorts of purposes.

Because that's just the way we are! Unlike artificial language models, no one programmed us to always be "helpful" or "innovative." Over time, however, we've become quite good at deciding what is worth preserving, as I explained in "WIE WIR ERZÄHLEN ...". I also reminded you in "ERKENNBAR, VERSTÄNDLICH, WÄHLBAR ..." that you are already part of the greater whole! You never speak solely for yourself but always for a part of humanity that feels just as you do. Furthermore, what does all of this have to do with democracy.

So why a Volume III?

I must admit, even I was surprised at first. I thought I was done. But no. The more I observed people's joy and reluctance in engaging with AI models, the more I looked at my leftover notes and realized: *WRITING...* there's still something there. We need to talk about it!

Sure, I could have turned this into a podcast or a *TikTok* video, giving you the flexibility to access it anytime, anywhere. But that wouldn't change the fact that I control the arrangement of the information, and you follow the presentation. Changing the medium doesn't alter much about the production process — as vividly illustrated in "*T2*" — released two decades after *Trainspotting.* One thing is clear: everything starts with scribbled notes.

Some things have changed in the last decades. People have been grouped into "Generation X, Y, Z..." and so on, leaving *old white men* and their female counterparts scratching their chins in confusion. Meanwhile, the younger, work-life-balancing generations are learning some grim truths: the planet is on the brink, democracy is struggling to hold its ground, and human rights?

Human rights were written down in 1948 by some well-meaning minds who decided for the whole world, and yet the whole world doesn't seem to care much.

Was Socrates right all along? That writing weakens memory and replaces true knowledge with mere recollection? That shallow knowledge blocks true wisdom and clouds our awareness? Today, we don't need to remember much — our countless digital assistants do it far better. So why not let them handle the writing as well?

There is an organization in Germany, the German armed forces *Bundeswehr*, that considers writing to be a form of corrective discipline. Tragic, isn't it? And if this (If you haven't served?) reminds you of your own school days, you probably know where the damage might have started.

How is it that the very same institution that taught us the cultural technique of reading and writing often managed to bullshit the joy of it at the same time?

Yes, you read that correctly. I used the verb 'bullshit' in a discussion on language. Which makes it clear that what you're holding in your hands is unmistakably human work, even though the book market offers you thousands of polished reading options lovingly patched together by some crafty *ChatGPT user.** Language models are not supposed to use inappropriate language — probably for the better!

AI enthusiasts warn us boldly: "Shit in, shit out." If you do not understand how to use language with nuance, you will get plenty of unsatisfying results spilling out of the digital interface. Frustration seems to be a built-in feature, but this time, the users are debugging. "Writing is so yesterday; today it's TikTok," teenagers protest as they push back against the drudgery of school. Well, in that case, >yesterday< must have been one long day!

Experts studying the opportunities and risks of artificial intelligence warn us: the ignorant will grow even more ignorant, while the clever will become even cleverer. Education creates elites? Is that a groundbreaking revelation? News of the world? No, just the same old story. Again? All quiet on the Western front.

"Democracy is the oligarchy of those who have time," wrote Paul Nolte in 2003, criticizing a system that relies heavily on voluntary engagement. By 2024, no one doubts anymore that unequal access to participation distorts democratic ideals. The "less-informed segment of the population" is seen as part of the problem by politically active individuals. Every day, we all struggle to interpret the flood of information available to us.

Writing a book that urges readers not to write a book might seem paradoxical. Maybe I just wanted to confuse the algorithms a little, who knows? Neuroscientists remind us that confusion is good for our synapses. It activates those tiny cells we carry around in our heads and kick-starts learning processes. And learning is always a good thing, isn't it? Whether for humans or machines.

Neuroplasticity proves that our brains are shaped by learning throughout our lives. Isn't *lifelong learning* and *education for all* less of a burden and more of an opportunity?

So, let's take a closer look at the process of writing and why this *cultural technique* is so essential for how we live together.

A picture is worth a thousand words — so why do we write? The images we like to praise with such a phrase are, after all, man-made. Do they differ so fundamentally from the letters we invented?

Images affect us as a whole, offering multiple interpretations, captivating us, and making themselves easy to remember. Why? Because they find countless points of connection in our minds, always already emotional, as it were. Otherwise, wouldn't they just be a quarter of an ink bottle spilled on a piece of paper?

But at some point, it was not enough for humanity to paint a picture on a cave wall. Faced with mortality, people sought to pass on their knowledge — the ever-expanding knowledge of humankind. So far, so familiar, you might think. The invention of writing hardly needs to be glorified, after all. Initially, as far as we can tell, it mainly served to record taxes and levies. And what does that have to do with democracy? Oh, everything!

Humans are storytellers. It is our unique ability to encode knowledge into stories and thereby pass on the capacity for survival from one generation to the next. Even today, one can observe how oral societies among indigenous tribes preserve their knowledge, often closely tied to the natural authority of elders. Spiritual leaders frequently held an advantage in knowledge and controlled what they passed on, safeguarding it through the power of hierarchy. Hardly democratic, right? Knowledge was not equally accessible — it was shared orally and only entrusted to select individuals.

It wasn't until the invention of writing that these dependencies began to change. For the system of writing, scribes have always been required, as mastering this craft — then and now — has been labor-intensive and time-consuming. This led to the emergence of an entirely new category of citizens: documentators and tax collectors, who were responsible for handling the writing and administrative tasks of their rulers.

> *"It is a sad chapter in the long history that began when some of us learned to read, while others among us continued to build structures and create wondrous things, thinking differently from the rest."*
>
> Maryanne Wolf,
>
> *"Proust and the Squid: The Story and Science of the Reading Brain,"*
>
> Chapter 'Conclusion': From the Reading Brain to 'What Comes Next'

The 'rest' — those illiterate or only partially capable of reading and writing — actually made up more than 90 percent of the population for thousands of years. They had to rely on orally transmitted knowledge to get by. After all, collective survival never really lost its appeal.

Today, one can detect that learning to write, and particularly the act of reading, has fundamentally changed the way our brains process thoughts, perhaps even permanently altering how our brains function altogether.

Humans, as multidimensional beings, sometimes display a notable tendency toward murder and mayhem. So, what's the big deal about the fact that the earliest written records in human history are tax documents? Figuring out, "How much does that guy owe me for keeping him safe?" is, after all, just another way of ensuring survival. Managing taxes, contributions, and supplies reflects a basic human need: order and control.

It was a first step toward creating mutual respect among humans. After all, it's hard to organize a fair trade when no one can remember who harvested how much. **Humans are gifted** with the ability to direct their thinking toward the future, the past, and the imaginary, **and writing seems to be an excellent medium for this.**

When things went well, humans were no longer entirely at the mercy of their rulers' whims. Rules and laws aided impulse control and provided a framework for reliability — one that allowed large groups of people to live together. When things didn't go so well... well, we can read all about that in our history books. Today, that is. Because there were people before us who made the effort to write their experiences down for us.

As early as 399 BCE, the Greek philosopher Plato recounted the skepticism of his teacher Socrates toward writing down knowledge. Socrates feared the superficiality of written words, which he regarded as *mute*. In his view, writing could not answer questions or spark genuine discussion. He also believed that writing weakened the memory. Knowledge not carried in the mind, he argued, was nothing more than an illusion. The idea that writing would allow more people to communicate across space and time was, for him — living in an age when few could write but nearly everyone could speak — utterly inconceivable. Plato's engagement with Socrates, however, went *viral*, as we might say today.

His writings, and other early texts like them, paved the way for something far greater. Suddenly, ideas could be preserved. Philosophy, science, religion — everything that had previously been passed down solely through spoken words was not just transmitted but conserved. With just two dozen symbols, the knowledge of the world was written down and made accessible to others.

The discourse around symbols might lead us to believe it shaped a community of intellectually free and equal individuals. But such a community did not exist. As long as learning to read and write remained a privilege reserved for those who needed it to make a living, there was no such thing as education for all.

Perhaps this was also because the literate were regarded with a certain suspicion by those who were not. Engaging with taxes, inventory management, and the rules of coexistence — essentially the *life-to-be* — the intermediate space where learning happens, fundamentally changes how people approach the realities of daily life.

As newborns, we are naturally inclined toward cooperation, living fully in the present moment, reacting to our environment spontaneously and unfiltered. Scribes, by contrast, seemed to represent the exact opposite. And so, with the establishment of new hierarchies and social classes, considerable effort was made to keep the spheres of human life strictly separate.

>Wer schreibt, der bleibt< "Publish or perish," claims Wikipedia, describing it as an outgrowth of the modern scientific enterprise. Perhaps. But in my mind's eye, I see wooden letters carved above the scriptorium of a monastery. People who, for centuries, earned their daily bread as copyists — because even a monastery needed income. Alas, I have no evidence to back this up. Wood, after all, weathers so quickly.

SCRIBO ERGO SUM

Others attribute it to the Roman statesman Caius Titus, who is said to have proclaimed this in the Roman Senate. Were we there? Hardly. And yet, I can picture him clearly in my mind's eye. My mind's eye — fascinating, isn't it?

Maryanne Wolf reminds us that nothing we write down is more important than what the reader can discover between the lines.

We learn through experience but we can also learn through the experiences of others. All we have to do is read them. In the moment we decode letters, thoughts take shape, and our consciousness changes. You could call it *deep learning*!

Did the invention of the printing press change everything for the better? Some things did, but not necessarily right away. Pamphlets, much like early newspapers, could be distributed widely. This made it easier to reach people in their daily lives and to contribute to the formation of public opinion. But too much opinion with too little knowledge is dangerous. It was not until after the Thirty Years' War in Europe, a catastrophe that wiped out nearly one-third of the population, that an awareness of the need for greater understanding began to emerge.

Shaped by his experiences in Latin school, Comenius yearned for a different kind of learning: education for all. For him, knowledge was no longer a privilege reserved for the few but a sacred right that belonged to all human beings. He envisioned a world (in his mind's eye) where everyone had access to knowledge.

Universität Lausanne AZ 1096 Res. A. **Reprint** ISBN 9781293477335

Orbis Sensualium Pictus, Abr. ed. 82 Pages, Johann Amos Comenius

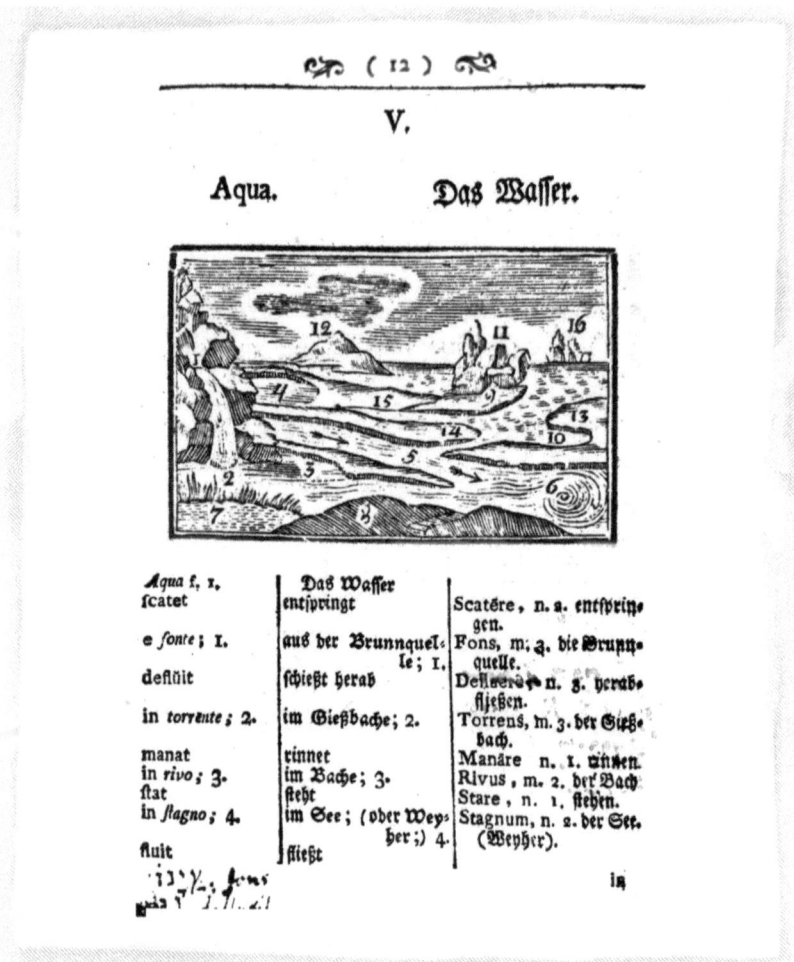

His work *Orbis Sensualium Pictus* revolutionized the European approach to education. Teaching eager learners, he believed, should be visual and self-directed. By combining terms and pictures to make the learning process more vivid and comprehensible, he forever changed how concepts and categories were conveyed across multiple languages — well into the age of Humanism.

First edition published in 1658; this edition dates after 1756, with handwritten additions of Hebrew and Latin words by a user.

(**13**)

h *flumĭne*; 5.	im Strome; 5	Flumen, n. 3. der Strom.
gyrátur	drehet sich	Gyráre, a. 1. sich drehen.
in *vortĭce*, 6.	im Wirbel; 6.	Vortex, m. 3. der Wirbel.
facit *palúdes*. 7.	machet Sümpfe. (Moräste) 7.	Palus, f. 3. der Sumpf. (Moraß).
Flumen n. 3. habet *ripas*. 8.	Der Fluß hat Ufer 8.	Ripa, f. 1. das Ufer am Flusse.
Mare n. 3. facit *liĕtŏra*, 9.	Das Meer machet Gestade, 9.	Littus, n. 3. das Gestade. (Ufer am Meere).
finus, 10.	Meerbusen, 10.	Sinus, m. 4. der Meerbusen.
promontorĭa, 11.	Vorgebirge, 11.	Promontorĭum, n. 2. das Vorgebirge.
infŭlas, 12.	Inseln, (Eylande,) 12.	Infŭla, f. 1. die Insel.
peninfŭlas, 13.	Halbinseln, 13.	Peninfŭla, f. 1. die Halbinsel.
ifthmos, 14.	Erdengen, 14.	Ifthmus, m. 2. die Erbenge. (das enge Land zwischen zweyen Meeren).
freta; 15.	Meerengen;(Sunde;) 15.	Fretum, n. 2. die Meerenge. (Sund).
et hab et *fcopŭlos* 16.	und hat Steinklippen. 16.	Scopŭlus, m. 2. die Steinklippe.

מָנוֹ *manu*
רִינוֹ *rinu*
אֲגַם *ftagnum*
נָהַר *flumen*
חָתַם *vortex*
בָּצָה *Palus*
שָׂפָה *littus*
חֵיק *finus*
בְּנִין *ieminĕa?*

אִי *infula*.

אִשְׁתַּבִיר *ifthmus*

יֵשׁ *deus, fcopulus*

VI.

In his vision, students were not meant to be passive recipients of knowledge but active participants engaging with the material. The handwritten notes in Hebrew demonstrate that this multilingual concept worked across borders.

And for those reminded of today's social media screenshots on *Facebook & Co.*, well, their mind's eye might not be mistaken.

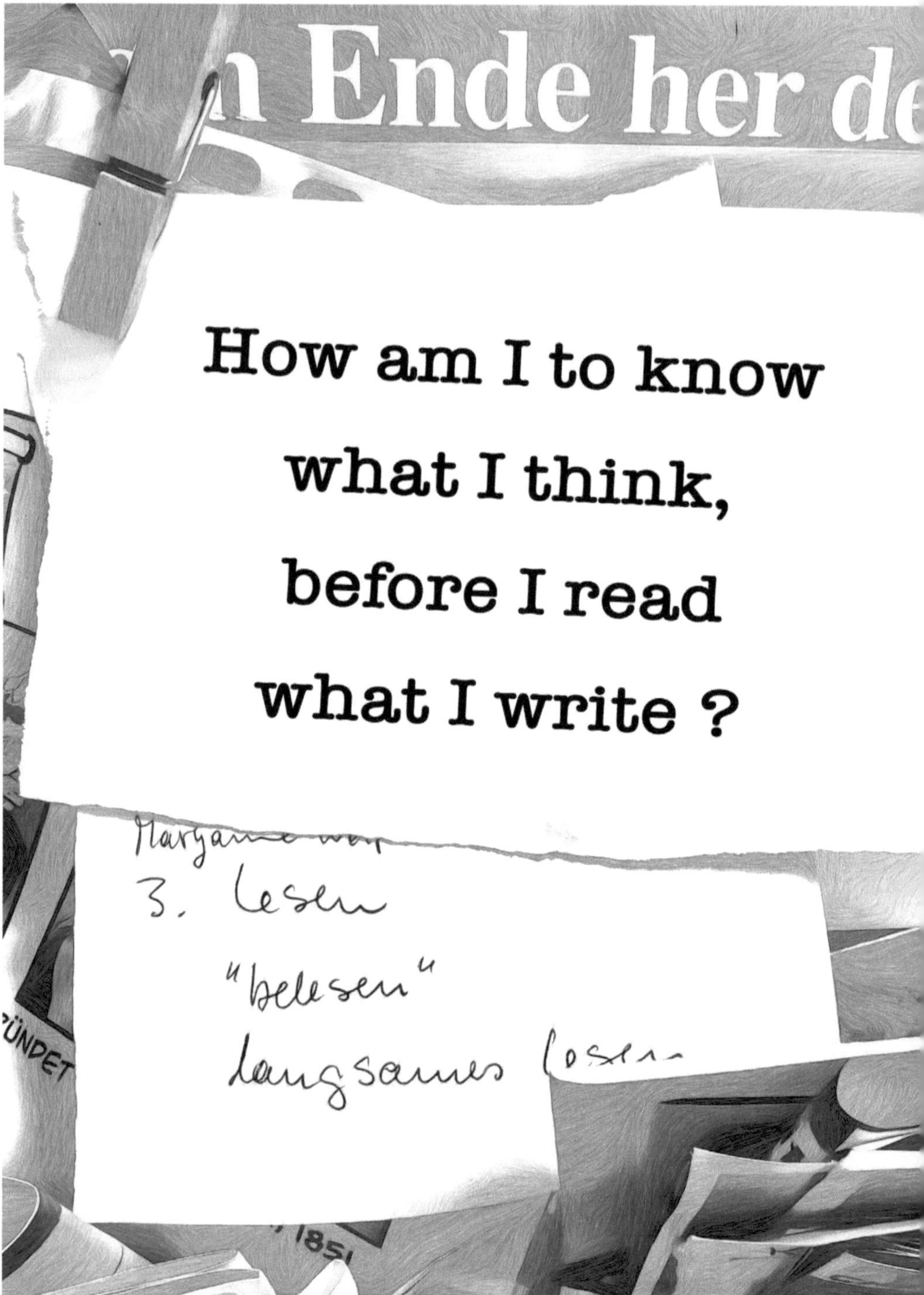
Ende her
How am I to know
what I think,
before I read
what I write ?
3. Lesen
"belesen"
langsames
ÜNDET
1851

When we all learned to write — a laborious task that went hand in hand with learning to read, thanks to our school education — we heard the phrase more than once: "Someone has to be able to read that!" Early on, we were made aware that what we write down can matter. If only, at first, to earn a decent grade on our essay and stay within the class average. Writing helps us think backwards from where we want to end up.

Putting our pen to paper demands a new kind of reflection from us. Like a sculptor, we must be able to envision the finished piece in our mind's eye. What seems like a simple exercise with a pencil forces us to structure our thoughts, keep the goal in sight, and plan backward. It is the ultimate act of slowing down — one that tests the patience (and stamina) of all young people.

Studying *Orbis Pictus*, the very book with which even Kant and Goethe learned as boys, inevitably brings us to Humanism. Translators and readers, copying texts from far-off languages, had already begun collecting their thoughts in commentaries. With the printing press, writers' ideas could finally reach both contemporaries and future generations. And in places where people with even more stamina gathered together — schools and universities — these ideas were eagerly expanded upon.

The Napoleonic ideas — ending the so-called God-willed feudal order, forging the French Revolution into the First Empire, and spoiling Europe with the Code Civil — once again forced society to rethink *actio* $\rightleftarrows$ *reactio*. Modern life, after all, demanded not only bailiffs and hygiene but also greater organization. Knowledge became power, ensuring the coexistence of many can succeed. Civil servants had the experience needed to implement rules within any state structure.

The invention of book printing did not, on its own, make knowledge available to everyone. In the 16th century, when Martin Luther translated the Bible into the German native tongue, it was more than just a religious matter. It was a political act that stirred social unrest. While a few German Bible translations already existed, Luther's version was deliberately crafted to be clear and familiar to everyone. He used a clear, colloquial language that could reach people from diverse backgrounds. The 'Book of Books' was no longer reserved for scholars but was now accessible to anyone who could read — and wanted to. The spread of Luther's Bible played a decisive role in advancing literacy among the population. The synodal principle of shared governance within the reformed church — that each individual ought to fulfill their duty to God by strengthening their reason through its diligent exercise — laid an essential cornerstone for what we now understand as personal autonomy and democracy.

Estimated Literacy Rates (hist. Sources):

17th century   est. 5-10 % (men) and 1-2 % (women)
                    mainly in cities or religious contexts

18th century   est. 10-20 % (men) and 5-10 % (women)

Around 1800   est. 25-35 % (men) and 10-20 % (women)

Literacy rose from the 18th century due to religious texts and pamphlets but remained limited to cities and the wealthy. Widespread literacy emerged in the 19th century with state-mandated schooling.

The shift of education came in the 19th century, as Napoleon's reforms crept through Europe. The *Code Civil*, introduced by Napoleon, required a clear legal framework and a more extensive administration, which could only be achieved through a literate population. Mandatory schooling and the expansion of public education were critical steps in preparing the population to meet these new demands. After all, a society growing increasingly complex required citizens capable of understanding contracts, reading laws, and actively participating in political processes.

The brothers Jacob and Wilhelm Grimm created works that would soon become staples in every household: first and foremost their *Children's and Household Tales* and eventually the *German Dictionary*. Literacy rates steadily increased, granting more people access to reading and writing.

The humanist ideal of 'education for all,' proclaimed during the Enlightenment, became a practical necessity for a modern state. If knowledge is power, then sharing this power was essential to creating a functioning, peaceful, and civilized society. The often war-driven enforcement of reforms to restructure the administration of conquered territories and to promote the citizen as an informed participant in the state eventually led to reading and writing becoming accessible not just to a privileged few but to the broader population. And with that, the proverbial *Pandora's Box* — once opened — ushered in change with far-reaching consequences.

A chorus of voices arose, demanding more democracy and participation. People began to see themselves as citizens and sought to establish a counterweight to the officials who, for centuries, had acted as the administrative power under every form of governance. The goal was to gain greater influence and a voice in decision-making, and to develop a system that did not rely solely on authority.

Although the democratic movement of 1848 ultimately failed, and the monarchy was poised to regain strength, the intellectual groundwork for Germany's later parliamentary constitutions had been laid. Amid all these changes, the written word grew increasingly significant. The political debates that had once taken place on the streets now moved into the private sphere. Letter writing gained such significance that we owe it to enterprising relatives, who brought these correspondences to publishers, that many of them have been preserved for us to admire even today.

Since Gutenberg invented the printing press in the mid-15th century, publishers had played a pivotal role — not only in distributing literary works but also in spreading political writings and pamphlets that informed people about important knowledge and ideas. As the audience for printed materials expanded, the significance of publishers grew alongside it.

Those in power have, at all times, taken an interest in the question: Who controls the knowledge distributed in printed form? By the 19th century, the first laws were introduced to regulate the book market.

Copyright laws provided publishers with a framework to ensure control over the distribution and sale of books and writings. With the exclusive rights granted to publishers for the works they printed, they were expected to protect their 'investment' and secure a stable financial foundation. Suddenly, the survival of publishing houses seemed more important than the intellectual property of the authors. So much for the idea of an 'author's right.' A well-mannered law, whose very name "Urheberrecht" in German remains misleading to this day. For authors, it often meant less influence over the distribution of their works. Thus began a balancing act between economic stability and artistic freedom.

Of course, it would be overly one-sided to merely scoff at the publishers' struggle to survive amidst fierce competition. Publishing houses like C. H. Beck and Ullstein — just to name two — produced significant works that shaped the political and social development of an emerging Germany and ensured their distribution. Moreover, economically stable publishing houses had the means to act as *patrons*, supporting talents who lacked access to noble networks of influence.

An editorial system began to take shape, allowing texts to be thoroughly reviewed, revised, and collaboratively improved, ultimately benefiting the relevance and resonance of new publications. Publishers amplified voices that might otherwise have gone unheard. The call for press freedom gained powerful advocates and became inseparably linked to the democratic movement of the 19th century.

Today, 65,000 new book titles are published in Germany each year. That's nearly 180 books per day, if you can imagine. If an average person reads about 30 pages per hour, it would take over 1,800 hours, or more than 75 days without pause, just to read the books published in a single day. The book market is so productive that even the most diligent readers can no longer keep up. It is hardly surprising, then, that publishers feel they already sufficiently represent the creative freedom of writers and have little patience — or sympathy — for self-publishing.

Even though reading habits are already shifting in the digital age, the average citizen of today's Federal Republic of Germany owns around 60 books. Of course, some own several hundred, while many others have far fewer. But just during their school years, young people handle an average of up to 50 books. It wasn't always this way!

With the rise of literacy and a growing appetite for reading, lending libraries made books accessible. And yet, making oneself comfortable with a good book wasn't as easy as one might think. It was not until the 1920s that electric light became common in private households, making it easier to read after a long day's work. Why do I even mention this? At the end of the 19th century, the average workday was 11 hours long. Anyone who wanted to immerse themselves in the pages of a book in the evening needed a great deal of inner calm and leftover energy — or the privilege of being able to read as part of their profession. Many instead opted for newspapers, which were easier to consume alongside other activities. Their market had exploded since the invention of the rotary press.

Over 3,500 different newspaper titles competed for the attention of their eager readership! Publishers increasingly recognized the diverse needs of specific target audiences, whose appetite for reading was to be sustained with a variety of genre offerings. Serialized stories became immensely popular, captivating even the most fatigued minds. Short and gripping, they provided brief escapes from the routine of everyday life, offering readers a momentary pause.

Wilhelm Busch, a talented illustrator and poet, paved the way for many who would follow him. With his masterful strokes and witty rhymes, he placed his stories as serialized features in newspapers, which were only later bound between book covers. His humorous illustrated tales — like the famous *Max and Moritz* — eventually found a permanent home on the bookshelves of the young German nation and far beyond its borders.

The light, entertaining nature of the newspaper provided the perfect platform to introduce readers to something new. After all, everything we read has the power to change our consciousness.

In no other author did imagination and self-perception blend as intensely as in the works of Karl May. With his travel novels, he achieved worldwide fame despite countless obstacles. All of them began as serialized stories in various newspapers, often published under different pseudonyms — let's be honest — to rake in a bit more cash. The many narrative threads leading to *Der Schatz im Silbersee* attained cult status, inevitably provoking both critics and envious detractors. And rightly so, for May was a complex personality — how we might politely put it today — and there's no shortage of people who would gladly *cancel* his legacy.

An author who presented himself to his fans as identical to his main character, *Old Shatterhand* — also known as *Kara Ben Nemsi* — would never get away with such a ruse today. Yet this very deception is what made Karl May so unique in his time. He lived his stories and portrayed himself with such conviction that he swept his readers away to distant worlds. The fact that he had never actually seen the lands of his most famous tales before writing about them hardly mattered. What he wrote were deeply felt adventures in which May captured the longings of his contemporaries for freedom and faraway places.

Through his self-stylization, the boundaries between fiction and reality began to blur. In doing so, he manipulated his followers much like his self-created character the "*Mübarek*" from *Der Schut* once did.

>Worte waren ursprünglich Zauber< "Words were originally magic" as Sigmund Freud once observed. The ability to write is a form of power capable of achieving great things. Yet it took two world wars and many missteps before we could arrive at the enlightened and critical readership that we nowadays take for granted.

It's not just when my children stand there today, bewildered by the sheer number of books in my parents' house, that I find myself helplessly shrugging: "There was no Internet!" How we ever found time for reading, talking, playing board games, and even watching TV regularly leaves *Digital Natives* utterly puzzled. How are you supposed to explain that: A world before the Internet? And why would you?

Luckily, the two of them got to spend a lot of time with their grandmother, experiencing the undivided attention of someone who could focus on them 100%. That kind of dedication is something you'd usually only find in a novel — or in a diary. Writing a diary? That's where today's youth completely checks out. There's probably an app for that by now, isn't there?

With an average of seven hours of screen time per day, we've been diligently feeding the learning language models of artificial intelligence via social media for years now. We experience this as interactive: *Comenius* meets *Sturm und Drang*! Blog posts and the linguistic compression they require demand a high level of creativity from us. Early on, I actively promoted the idea of not leaving *Facebook & Co.* to those who don't have democracy's best interests at heart.

The internet inevitably sharpens our ability to engage in discourse, while unfiltered spaces expose the abyss of what freedom of speech can become. Due to this, however, the ability to string together subject, verb, and object is slipping away from more and more people. Yet data engineers do have access to everything ever written by those before us. So at least *ChatGPT* still speaks to us in full sentences — or rather, writes. Remember: The only reason we can read at all is because those who came before us wrote down their experiences and ideas. And their feelings!

My mother did not write much in her lifetime, but no one could craft letters and greeting cards quite like she did. Cards in which she knew how to express her feelings with words that truly touched the heart. When I was little, she regularly made us write postcards on vacation. She taught me the concept: drafting first, minding the line spacing, checking for relevance — writing not just for the sake of it, but with purpose! To this day, I still have countless cards from that era, carefully kept in my home. It's incredible how much effort she put into reaching people with words, opening a window to attention and love.

Beyond the grand organization of humanity and its neural networks, Mike Mandl draws our attention to the profound impact a single thought can have on any thinking, feeling human being:

> **"A human being is a multidimensional entity, a layered unity that is far more than the sum of its functions. We are a dynamic system, constantly in relationship with and in exchange with our surroundings. [...]**
>
> **Just like our bodies, our hearts, minds, and souls need nourishment — substances that sustain them and keep them alive. [...]**
>
> **We need love, we need enthusiasm, we need meaning. And we seek it. [...]**
>
> **We need feeding on every level of our being. Otherwise, despite a full stomach, an inner emptiness remains."**
>
> *translated from Mike Mandl, "Meridiane - Landkarten der Seele," pp. 18-24*

A single thought can awaken our vital spirits.

Whenever I stubbornly told my mother, "I don't know what to write!" she would send me out for a walk. And, almost magically, thoughts would arrange themselves effortlessly. The research of Opezzo and Schwartz at Stanford University suggests that walking isn't just good for family dynamics from time to time — it also significantly enhances cognitive performance and creativity.

With rhythm and breath, our gaze expands into the distance, allowing us to see the bigger picture while simultaneously noticing the smallest details. This interplay between macroscopic vastness and microscopic precision creates space for clarity and new ideas.

At the very least, I managed to fill the blank spaces of my postcards meaningfully. And to this day, I have a soft spot for linguistic compression. Good writing requires both stamina and movement!

These invitations to reflect on what is good in our lives are something I still hold dear. My mother was exceptional at the things she did and knew exactly what she didn't want: for instance, to write a book. One of her firmest nudges was always, "I know you can do this even better." So I keep pushing myself, striving not to disappoint her posthumously, with my determined attempt to illuminate the connection between our talent for writing and language and our capacity for genuine cooperation and democracy through 'education for all.'

What and how much we should write has been our concern since elementary school. We learn to express ourselves in different formats and to meet *genre* expectations. Plenty of people dream of writing their own book — but does that still make sense? Will AI soon be doing all the writing anyway, leaving us free to just sit back and relax? Because, let's be honest, we all remember this from school: writing is demanding. It takes effort, focus, and time. So why do it at all?

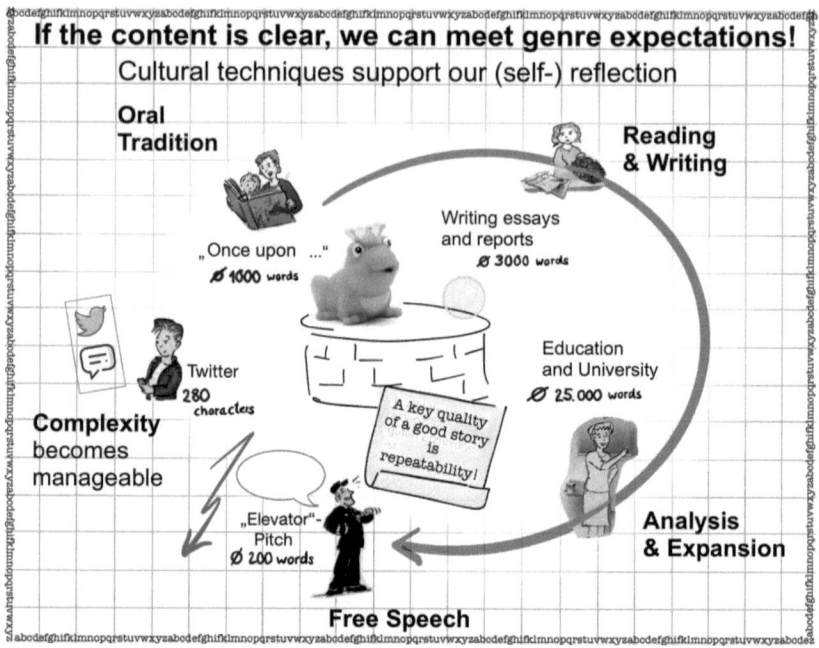

If the content is clear, we can meet genre expectations!
Cultural techniques support our (self-) reflection

Oral Tradition

Reading & Writing

Writing essays and reports
Ø 3000 words

„Once upon ..."
Ø 1000 words

Twitter
280 characters

Education and University
Ø 25.000 words

A key quality of a good story is repeatability!

Complexity becomes manageable

„Elevator"-Pitch
Ø 200 words

Analysis & Expansion

Free Speech

We learn to master a variety of cultural techniques in school and further education. The ability to navigate between formats and genres strengthens our (self-)reflection. Through the diversity of forms, we learn to view our thoughts from different angles and find creative solutions. If we know the content of *The Frog Prince*, we can describe this narrative motif in countless ways. This flexibility in thinking deepens our understanding of ourselves and the world around us. After all, the effort of 'reading - writing - reading' has to pay off somehow, doesn't it?

Both the process of learning to read and write, as well as reading itself, take time. Time that is no longer available for other things. Clear structures seemingly enhance understanding. After all, let's not forget what it's all for: survival — as a group!

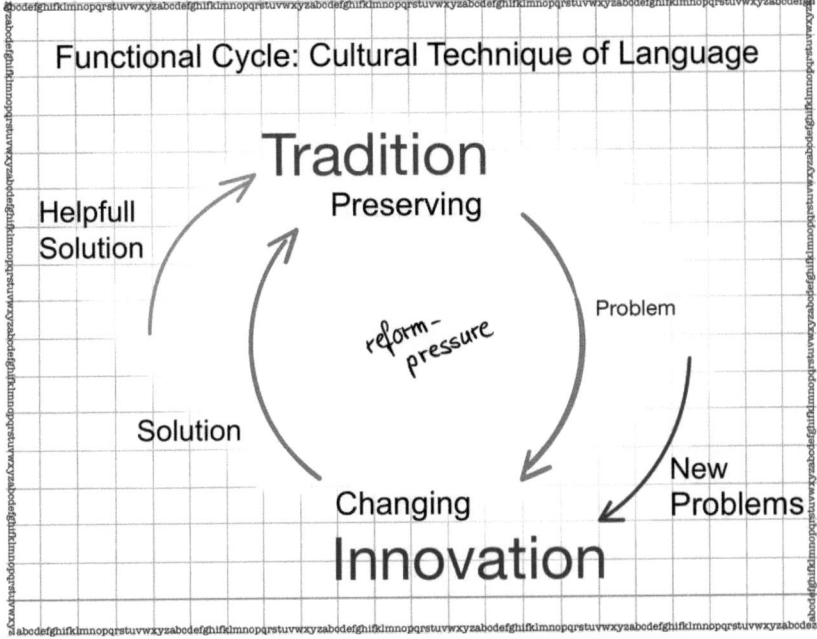

Everything we describe is to be found in the tension between preservation and progress. As a learning organization >humanity< we carefully consider what is worth carrying forward as part of our traditions. Cultural techniques are not just useful tools for individuals; they have evolved as collective practices that connect us. Impressive, isn't it? Yet for many — not just Socrates — this also evokes unease. Niklas Luhmann points out that communication is always selective, as we can never fully control the meaning of our words. This only amplifies the discomfort of written exchange.

When we hesitate while writing, we are always accompanied by uncertainty: How will the teacher, the recipient of our letter or postcard — or any reader, for that matter — interpret the meaning of our words?

In spoken dialogue, we can immediately adjust to our conversation partner's understanding. In writing, however, encountering — or intentionally stretching — expectations (an experience you've surely had yourself) helps us connect with strangers. So, despite all the stamina it requires, is writing actually a 'hot medium'?

Anyone who has ever written a job application knows the challenge: meeting the expectations for such a letter while still standing out from the flood of applications to secure a real chance at an interview. Suddenly, letters and numbers make information seem comparable. Yet behind every application stands a human being, a unique creature expressing their fundamental need for connection and participation. The format itself can sometimes make all the difference.

So, we must not drown in expectations or merely reproduce familiar patterns. As pleasant as boredom can be — a state that both challenges the brain and often creates space for new neural connections — we still need to break free from routine and spark creative impulses to keep evolving. This also explains how genres shift over time. After all, they are never static but respond to the needs and expectations of their audiences.

Navigating daily life in pre-modern times, without central heating, electricity, or housing permits, demanded a great deal from people. Essential survival knowledge had to be easy to remember and almost unconsciously accessible. But life is not just about managing the present; it is also about preparing for the future. To prevent the many from relying solely on passive knowledge, the emergence of genres played a crucial role in facilitating exchange between artists and audiences. Throughout human history, genres have functioned as interfaces between preserved tradition and creative renewal, shaping how knowledge and ideas are passed down.

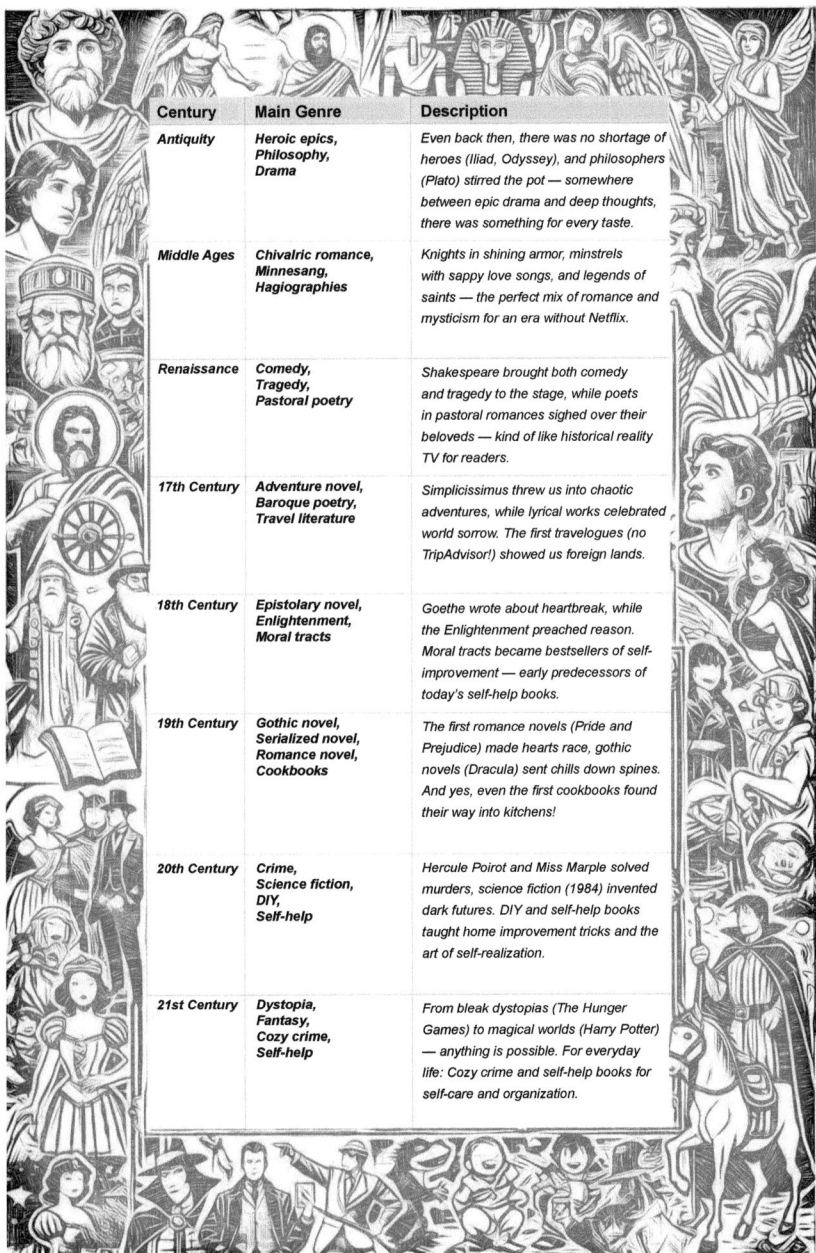

Century	Main Genre	Description
Antiquity	Heroic epics, Philosophy, Drama	Even back then, there was no shortage of heroes (Iliad, Odyssey), and philosophers (Plato) stirred the pot — somewhere between epic drama and deep thoughts, there was something for every taste.
Middle Ages	Chivalric romance, Minnesang, Hagiographies	Knights in shining armor, minstrels with sappy love songs, and legends of saints — the perfect mix of romance and mysticism for an era without Netflix.
Renaissance	Comedy, Tragedy, Pastoral poetry	Shakespeare brought both comedy and tragedy to the stage, while poets in pastoral romances sighed over their beloveds — kind of like historical reality TV for readers.
17th Century	Adventure novel, Baroque poetry, Travel literature	Simplicissimus threw us into chaotic adventures, while lyrical works celebrated world sorrow. The first travelogues (no TripAdvisor!) showed us foreign lands.
18th Century	Epistolary novel, Enlightenment, Moral tracts	Goethe wrote about heartbreak, while the Enlightenment preached reason. Moral tracts became bestsellers of self-improvement — early predecessors of today's self-help books.
19th Century	Gothic novel, Serialized novel, Romance novel, Cookbooks	The first romance novels (Pride and Prejudice) made hearts race, gothic novels (Dracula) sent chills down spines. And yes, even the first cookbooks found their way into kitchens!
20th Century	Crime, Science fiction, DIY, Self-help	Hercule Poirot and Miss Marple solved murders, science fiction (1984) invented dark futures. DIY and self-help books taught home improvement tricks and the art of self-realization.
21st Century	Dystopia, Fantasy, Cozy crime, Self-help	From bleak dystopias (The Hunger Games) to magical worlds (Harry Potter) — anything is possible. For everyday life: Cozy crime and self-help books for self-care and organization.

Genres, especially those in popular entertainment, have long been dismissed by those who considered themselves educated. It is no coincidence that terms like *Volksschwank* (folk farce) or *Volksweise* (folk tune) emerged, mere trifles for the masses, who supposedly had no need to engage with the weightier matters of life.

Yet, as literary genres developed, it became increasingly difficult for detractors to justify their condescension. After all, consuming and distributing these works required basic literacy skills. As early as the 18th century, Knigge urged his contemporaries to recognize the warmth and sincerity of so-called *simple people*, noting that "a simple soul sees better with the heart than many a refined court flatterer." Still, with the notable exception of Comenius, it was not until the modern era that light reading, comics, and even graphic novels were acknowledged as valuable tools for introducing the general public to the practice of reading.

More and more people were reading, while only a select few were writing — or so one might think. In reality, balancing competing interests in the face of steady population growth over the centuries required an ever-expanding bureaucracy. Thanks to universal education, citizens could increasingly be called upon to take part in the administration of municipal and tax affairs.

After World War II, typewriters and filing cabinets were no longer confined to government offices, they soon found their way into every private household. "Whose bread I eat, his song I sing," seemed to apply not only to monks in scriptoriums but to all of us. In a way, we have all become civil servants, managing the administration of our shared existence.

Self-governance has become part of civic consciousness — the ability to counter undue external control: with one's own structure, one's own records, one's own tax return.

Whether we're drafting a job reference, writing invoices, filing a tax return, or composing a thank-you note — we write, and write, and write, for an entire lifetime. And most of what we write disappears into some file folder or another.

For some, it's labeled >classified<, confidential, private, protected by data regulations. For others, it's marked business secret, patent, inventor's disclosure, or notarized document.

We write in both public and private spaces, believing — perhaps naively — that through our words, we are making this world just a little bit better.

Digitalization came as a relief to many, offering an escape from a job that consumed far too much time: being the bureaucrat of our own lives.

No one asked us before we were born whether we wanted to live in a country where nearly every breath we take must be documented. Where a workweek includes setting aside time to file bank statements, pay invoices, log trips and work hours — and take care of who knows how many other paperwork tasks this civilization has invented.

Since the unification of Germany in 1871, the postal monopoly was firmly held by the state, and a hundred years later, letter mail remained the primary mode of private and business communication. In West Germany alone, over 20 billion letters were sent annually — until the 1990s, when the fax machine paved the way for change.

Our passion for writing has created a bureaucracy monster.

As supposed heirs of the Enlightenment and Humanism that emerged from it, we like to think ourselves as *immune* to superstition and manipulation. But that hasn't always been the case. And since we've already examined the actual literacy rates of the 19th century back on page 20, allow me another detour — this time into a genre that continues to shape our television screens to this day: crime fiction.

Television? Exactly. We've already discussed *speaking images*, and I've mentally checked off the rise of film, television, and broadband with this simple remark: everything begins with a written — or, if you will, scribbled — piece of paper.

As an example, I would like to take a closer look at the rise of the crime genre, as it provides deep insight into fundamental human needs. As someone with a keen interest in cultural studies, I firmly believe that understanding the world before us is crucial to shaping the quality of the media landscape we create. After all, we are all cultural contributors — every single day that we think, speak, and write!

Rather than immediately diving into Edgar Allan Poe's brilliant detective figure, *Dupin*, whom he introduced in 1841, I would like to invite you to reflect on why the *dark side* of human nature holds such an enduring fascination for us. And, of course, what this might have to do with democracy. After all, every crime story revolves around the use of power and the social question of how we choose to handle it. The value of justice plays a crucial role, as does the ongoing development of our security structures, which we rely on to ensure a safe coexistence.

Since the dawn of humankind, we have been both fascinated and horrified by acts of murder and violence. Despite the fact that one of our most fundamental needs is survival, as we can observe in the cooperative nature of every newborn. That may sound like I am starting with Adam & Eve — why not? The 'Book of Books' — the Old Testament — already contains all the ingredients of the crime stories we still tell today. Betrayal, deception, power, and punishment; nothing new under the sun. Intellectual freedom and emancipation from power structures are akin to expulsion from paradise. And it took a few more centuries before someone dared to object: "Let him who is without sin cast the first stone!"

Crimes such as murder, betrayal, theft, and abuse of power are already depicted in the Bible, structured within a narrative logic of crime, motive, perpetrator, and punishment. These are the typical elements of every classic tale of horror and intrigue, retold beyond the written word.

Yet, if we imagine the cycle of 'reading – writing – reading' across generations, we realize that every author of the 19th and 20th centuries was familiar with these stories. And not just these. The demands of an increasingly interconnected society led writers like Evagrius Ponticus and Pope Gregory to reflect on the vices and corrupting thoughts that divide people — ideas later popularized by Thomas Aquinas under the term "the seven deadly sins."

No authority in the world can ensure peace among humankind if the individual does not take it upon themselves to confront their own inclinations toward pride, greed, lust, envy, gluttony, wrath, and sloth. Each of these traits, in its own way, may be endearing — part of what makes us human — but left unchecked, they can lead to certain ruin. Too much is too much, this was likely the thought of Jewish mystics around the year 1000 CE when they described the figure of *Lilith* in the *Alphabetum Siracidis*. In later interpretations, she was seen as Adam's first wife, one who refused to submit to a patriarchal order and defied both societal and divine authority. A true anti-heroine — we might say today — one perpetually at odds with the established order.

The ingredients of today's crime stories had long been carefully thought out and recorded. You may argue that what was still missing were television, the printing press, electric light, and widespread literacy to fuel the rise of the dime novel. But one more element was needed to propel crime fiction into mass popularity: industrialization!

For centuries, society had been bound by rigid class structures, but with the rise of industry, these certainties unraveled into shifting social milieus. The familiar rhythms of work and life were disrupted, and the trusted authorities of old no longer ensured justice and order. Most significantly, changing work schedules altered how people gathered and shared their lives. Language and storytelling, after all, have always served a function.

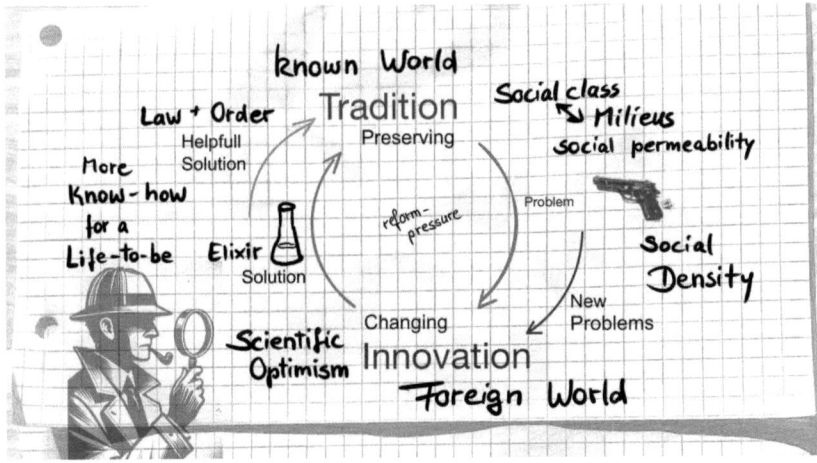

In the 19th century, the narrative of the *brilliant detective* took shape. Gone was the omniscient narrator who unveiled unseen truths. Now, it was a flesh-and-blood individual, relying solely on the keen application of knowledge. In an era of growing disorder, people found a sense of structure and security through individuals they could follow in thought, whose reasoning they could understand, and whose pursuit of truth made the world feel a little less uncertain.

By reading a detective story, one could not only partake in the modern knowledge of the investigator but also delve into the psyche of those involved. This provided an invaluable learning curve, fostering new social competencies and offering a brief escape from the fragmentation of daily life. And so, we all became undercover detectives, strolling — pleasurably and unseen — through unfamiliar milieus, preparing ourselves, in a way, for the *life-to-be*.

In the modern world, acquiring wealth became easier. But beyond riches, education and marriage also granted access to previously unfamiliar spheres, where one had to know how to conduct oneself. With newfound mobility came the need to navigate social environments no longer shaped by one's upbringing. The stability of one's status was no longer guaranteed; just as one could rise to wealth, one could just as easily fall into poverty — like the good *Dr. Watson* from Arthur Conan Doyle's *Sherlock Holmes* stories.

While Sherlock Holmes was a rather unsympathetic figure, met with suspicion and skepticism, Dr. Watson — despite his doctorate — embodied the kind of everyman one would gladly have as a neighbor. In this way, Doyle cleverly addressed the reservations people of his time had toward an excessive devotion to science. Together, the detective duo represented a balance: Watson's intuition and occasional superstition stood in contrast to Holmes's relentless logic and insatiable scientific curiosity.

Like any esteemed author, Arthur Conan Doyle wrote more than just the Sherlock Holmes stories. Yet through his creation of a clear narrative structure, one that compellingly depicted reason triumphing over chaos, he became a literary star. Weary of the relentless attention surrounding his character, Doyle killed off Sherlock Holmes in *The Final Problem* in 1893. However, public pressure grew so immense that he eventually resurrected Holmes. With that, the image of the perfect investigator — overwhelmingly intelligent, fiercely independent, and almost superhuman — was forever cemented in the collective consciousness.

Doyle used his public influence and passion for forensics and scientific investigation to engage in politics and social issues. In two cases, he applied the very methods of his fictional detective to help overturn wrongful convictions. In doing so, he played a key role in strengthening the *presumption of innocence* and exposing wrongful convictions. One of the most notable cases he brought to light was that of George Edalji. A young Anglo-Indian solicitor, whom Doyle firmly believed to be innocent, was wrongfully convicted in 1903 and sentenced to prison for allegedly mutilating livestock. Doyle conducted his own investigation, uncovering multiple errors in the evidence and demonstrating that Edalji had been convicted due to racial prejudice. Thanks to Doyle's relentless efforts, Edalji was exonerated in 1907.

The widespread coverage of Doyle's efforts played a significant role in the establishment of the *Court of Criminal Appeal* in 1907, an institution dedicated to reviewing miscarriages of justice. His personal involvement underscored the importance of the presumption of innocence and fair trial procedures, helping to restore confidence in the British legal system.

For the newspapers of his time, distinguishing between fiction and reality in the case of Arthur Conan Doyle and *Sherlock Holmes* proved remarkably difficult.

Holmes was portrayed with such realism that many readers — and even journalists — perceived him as a near-living figure. Reports surfaced of readers allegedly sending letters to *Holmes*, seeking his advice on real-life criminal cases.

This blending of fiction and reality intensified when Doyle became involved in actual investigations, such as the George Edalji case. Journalists, accustomed to maintaining clear distinctions between real-life individuals and literary characters, suddenly faced a phenomenon where those boundaries began to blur.

On one hand, people expected Doyle to behave like *Holmes*; on the other, many were baffled that the "rationalist" Doyle was also a fervent spiritualist. The genre's expectation of a brilliant yet cold logician clashed with the reality of Doyle as a far more complex and contradictory human being. Beyond the Holmes stories, Doyle also wrote *The Lost World*, featuring the equally captivating *Professor Challenger* as its central figure.

With this character — one who combined science, adventure, and controversial theories — Doyle overwhelmed many of his contemporaries, yet in doing so, he laid the groundwork for modern *science fiction* storytelling.

Challenger was a rebel, a fusion of scientist and adventurer, forever living in the shadow of *Holmes*. Yet, in his bold defiance of convention, he reflects the depth and foresight of his creator, who served as a literary seismograph of societal change. Doyle, an avid reader as well as a writer, was far less blindly devoted to science than he is often credited with posthumously.

The expectations of readers play a crucial role in the creation of literature, especially when it comes to formats, roles, and genres. Readers approach a work with predefined notions when they allow themselves the freedom to immerse in a particular genre. These expectations shape the way we perceive a story.

If a detective novel promises that the culprit will be revealed in the end, readers expect a logical resolution to the case. The same applies to character roles: in a crime story, the detective takes on the role of the problem solver, navigating within familiar genre conventions. When these expectations are deliberately fulfilled or skillfully stretched, it creates tension and intrigue, keeping readers engaged.

Reader expectations do act as an invisible contract between writer and audience — a kind of 'guideline' that shapes the creative process and influences how stories are consumed. They bring order to the vast diversity of literary works, offering both readers and writers a shared framework within which meaning is constructed and narratives unfold.

Yet it is precisely in this balance between expectation and innovation that writers find the opportunity to establish new narratives. By deliberately stretching genres or challenging traditional roles, they can surprise audiences and introduce fresh perspectives. As creators of culture, writers absorb the expectations of their time and evolve them into new storytelling structures. Arthur Conan Doyle did just that when, in his *Sherlock Holmes* stories, he not only embraced the classic detective archetype but also popularized scientific methods as a means of investigation. With *The Lost World*, he introduced a new narrative form 'science fiction' that blended adventure with scientific speculation. Innovations within formats create new literary trends and reshape the way readers think about and engage with the world. As to be continued.

Many political writings of this era, despite over 90% of the population in Britain and other Western countries being literate, read in a strikingly unenlightened manner. These works often propagated the so-called "natural" superiority of men over "the female sex," "other races," or entire subjugated regions. Views that were commonplace within the framework of European colonialism and imperialism. They defended claims to power and discriminatory forms of government while continuing to legitimize patriarchal structures. Such writings lagged far behind the social ideas explored in crime fiction, where issues of justice, order, and social mobility were tackled with conviction.

It becomes evident that fiction, precisely because of its entertaining nature, often reached a far wider audience and proved to be more forward-thinking than the so-called "serious" political debates of its time.

The feeling of being well entertained was accompanied by a sense of perceived interactivity: by solving crimes, fundamental questions of morality, law, and justice were brought into focus, allowing important societal issues to be negotiated indirectly. The often-dismissed escapism of the crime genre, rather than being mere distraction, placed individual responsibility and one's duty to society at the very center of the narrative.

A deeper understanding of roles, later articulated by Erving Goffman, helps us grasp the dynamics of social life. In a fragmented society, every individual must recognize that they do not embody just one role, but many — shifting between contexts as an employee or employer, family member, citizen, consumer, and more. Throughout human history, role assignments have shaped new expectations and responsibilities, varying depending on the environment.

The constant psychological and social interplay between professional, familial, and societal roles became a crucial factor for both individual and collective survival in the modern, industrialized world.

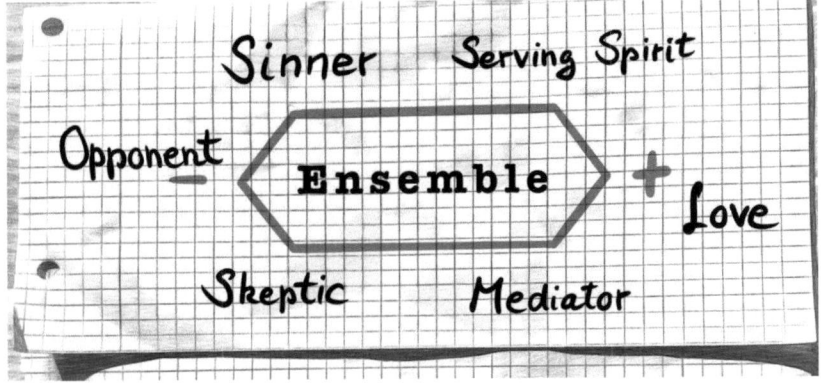

The ability to respond flexibly to these role expectations and to understand when and how to adapt became a key competence. This remains relevant to this day, as people must often navigate between their private lives and the public sphere to secure their livelihood. Role expectations grew increasingly complex, and a deeper understanding of these expectations helps individuals better interpret their own actions as well as those of others — and to respond accordingly.

Crime fiction is particularly well-suited to reflecting the role of the individual within society. Characters such as the detective or the culprit are deeply tied to specific social roles, and as an audience, we develop expectations based on these roles. Yet, just as in real life, there are moments in fiction when these roles are disrupted or subverted, prompting us to reconsider our own social roles and expectations.

Surely, you belong to the generations that learned to write essays and reports by answering the so-called W-questions in school and training. Why not? After all, thousands of newspaper editors rely on the same approach.

At first glance, the W-questions — Who, What, When, Where, Why, and How — seem like a reliable tool for structuring information and providing complete answers. However, if we limit ourselves to merely answering these questions, we risk capturing only the surface of a subject without truly grasping its depth. What we then lack is the ability to create meaning: to recognize the essence behind the facts.

While we might spend a ritualized half-hour "skimming" a newspaper — as my father likes to put it — it would take a person 8 to 10 hours to read a typical daily paper line by line. That's over 100,000 characters, crafted by media professionals who collectively invest around 200 working hours to shape them for print. This time includes researching, writing, editing, and fact-checking. In traditional newspaper production, additional hours were needed for layout, photography, and printing, significantly increasing the total effort required to produce a single edition.

The so-called W-questions may force us to gather information, but they do not automatically help us place that information into a meaningful context.

Experienced journalists, however, mastered their craft and, as early as the 19th century, contributed to significant democratization effects through their investigative approach.

Knowledge of grievances and abuses of power was thus made accessible to a broad audience. So much for the success story. But, as we know, every coin has two sides. With the recognition of the press as the "fourth estate" in a democracy — alongside the legislative, executive, and judicial branches — came the enduring myth that truly neutral reporting exists.

Nonsense! But that's the nature of narratives that flatter the vanity of the powerful — they're simply impossible to kill! Because newspapers held immense power long before — well, you know: the Internet came along.

No matter what medium you write for, free yourself from the illusion that you are reporting neutrally. No one can — even when carefully adhering to the W-questions — write with complete neutrality. Every selection of information, every turn of phrase, and every emphasis reflects a personal perspective. The W-questions (Who, What, When, Where, Why, How) may guide journalistic focus, but the interpretation of facts and the way words and letters are combined are always subjective. A writer's cultural, political, and social background inevitably influences their reporting, even when they strive for objectivity.

No wonder, then, that educated teachers tend to grade essays from children of academically educated parents more favorably. A writer's language acquisition shapes not only the (often unconscious) choices they make in content but also how their words are (unconsciously) perceived by the reader. It is not just the selection of facts but also how they are presented and interpreted that inevitably introduces a degree of subjectivity into any form of reporting. Neutrality, in this sense, remains a theoretical aspiration.

We should finally send the *sacred cow* of supposed neutrality off to the sanctuary and embrace the value of conscious perspective. Only by acknowledging our own uniqueness — shaped by life itself — can we communicate authentically.

Instead of striving for neutrality at all costs, becoming aware of our own biases — and reflecting on them — could help us make our perspective on the world more transparent and balanced. Only then can a truly informed discussion take place. One that does not pretend to be objective but consciously takes a stance.

But if we, as has happened all too often, merely 'describe' without reflecting, without offering food for thought between the lines, then readers do not truly read anymore; they merely skim. And in doing so, they risk overlooking the bigger picture. Doesn't that leave all of us blind to what truly matters?

One man who truly kept reading newspapers was Alfred Hitchcock. He often drew inspiration from small articles, picking up everyday stories of crime and mishaps and transforming them through his unique narrative style. Hitchcock was a master at building suspense by strategically withholding information from his audience while leading his characters into perilous situations. His stories were never neutral reports — they were deeply personalized explorations of human fears and weaknesses, always laced with irony.

Even in the screenplay stage, he had a way of captivating his production teams. He saw the script not just as a written plan, but as a functional tool — meant to align his team, shape performances, and translate his vision into moving images. Hitchcock often remarked that the real film was created in pre-production. The actual shooting, he claimed, was merely the execution of scenes he had already envisioned in his mind.

Hitchcock's writing process was a collaborative and creative act, where every word was carefully chosen to intensify suspense and shape atmosphere. To achieve this, he worked with some of the finest screenwriters of his time. His ability to transform everyday news into gripping narratives cemented his reputation as the "Master of Suspense." No mindless recitation of W-questions, just pure mystery.

Reading — and truly wanting to read — demands stamina and the energy to do nothing else. Many writers dream of weaving so much *suspense* into their texts that the reading process itself becomes effortless, carried by a delicate balance between building tension and skillfully presenting facts. Creating such a dynamic requires a deliberate interplay of information and expectation.

Hitchcock never let his readers or viewers simply check off facts or follow predictable resolutions. Instead, he crafted an atmosphere of constant uncertainty. Suspense wasn't just about *What happens next?* It was equally about *How?* and *Why?*

Mystery and uncertainty are essential to creating suspense in any reading process. Readers must be given enough information to follow along but never so much that they fully understand everything right away. This imbalance creates the pull that keeps them turning page after page.

The so-called W-questions can certainly play a role, but not as a simple checklist. Instead, they function as open-ended inquiries that remain dynamic throughout the narrative. If too much is resolved too quickly, the intrigue fades, and the eyes begin to skim rather than truly read. Until, yes, until, something *inconsistent*, something complex appears among the lines, demanding deeper attention once again.

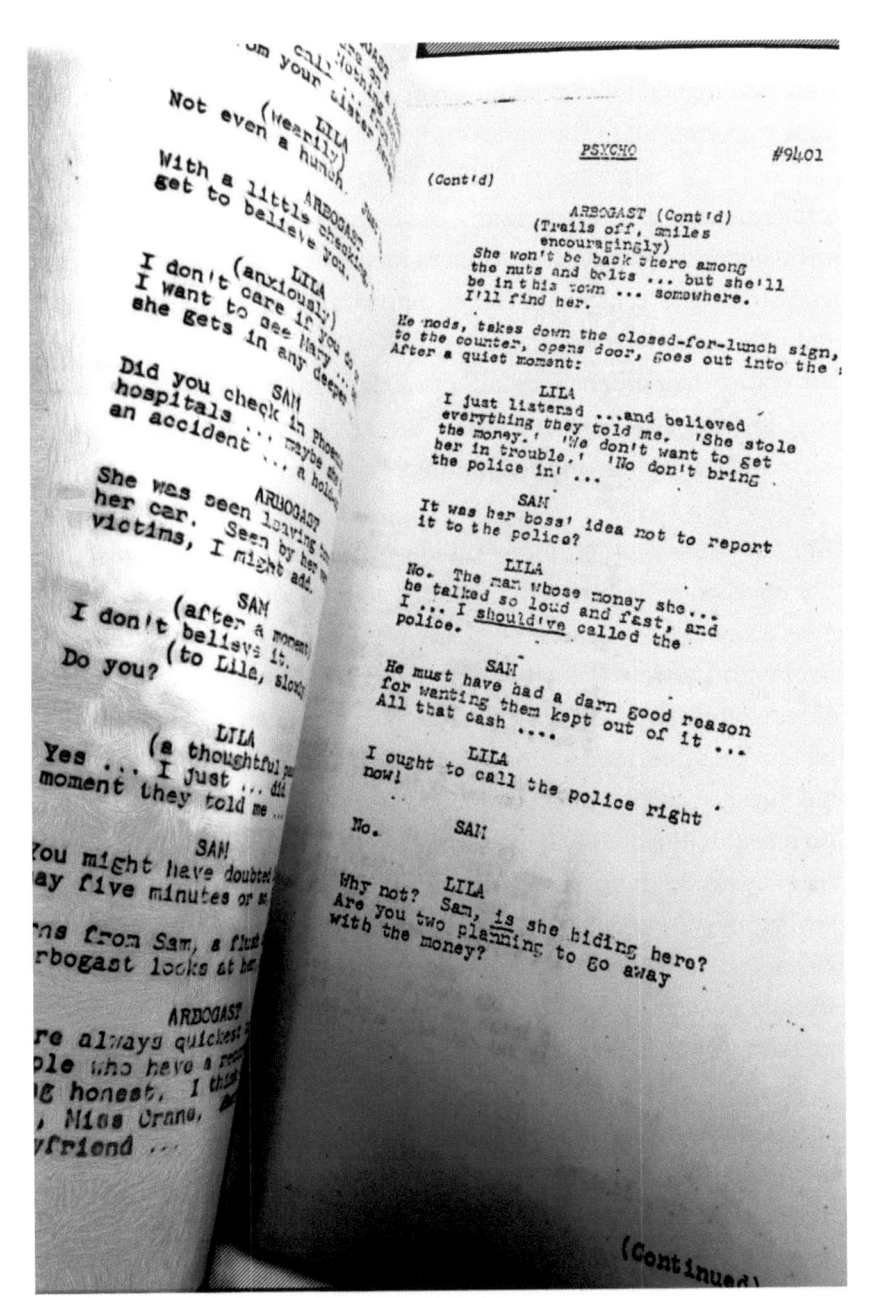

The skilled writer counts on the effectiveness of slow reading. 'Slow reading' is not just about savoring every word but about fully immersing oneself in the mood and structure of the text. Reading at a slower pace heightens the effect of suspense, forcing the reader to take their time absorbing the nuances of the writing. Much like in Hitchcock's films, where the camera slowly zooms in on a crucial detail until the tension becomes unbearable, a text that unfolds gradually can build even greater suspense. It is this controlled pacing that places the reader in a state of restless anticipation, compelling them to keep reading even when the answers remain just out of reach. Yet, the promise of resolution remains essential.

After the tabloid press, many online platforms have exploited this very effect to generate clicks without actually providing content of value. They toy with users' curiosity, only to disappoint them in the end. Instead of delivering answers or delving deeper into topics, the content often ends abruptly or remains superficial — leaving the audience not informed but outright punished for their curiosity. This does not just lead to frustration; it breaks trust, ultimately calling into question the quality of discourse itself.

Writers who skillfully employ suspense understand that readers and viewers love to speculate. We enjoy being left in the dark, as it gives us space for our own thoughts. They know that suspense must be carefully measured — enough to keep us engaged, but not so little that our interest fades.

Today, we spend an average of more than two hours a day following, reading, and scrolling through social media. Not in one sitting, but scattered throughout the day — unanswered comments and lingering questions keeping our curiosity alive.

This constant flood of information and the way we consume it have reshaped our expectations of content and genres. In the past — before there was internet — writing was often more rigidly bound to structured format expectations, much like 'paint by numbers.' In the 1980s, formulas and mass-produced content dominated many genres. But as daily life became increasingly overwhelming, new genre forms emerged to help us process this reality. Let's remind ourselves once more: genres like crime fiction or thrillers reflect humanity's deep-seated urge to create order from chaos. They are valuable not only because they entertain but because they help us find meaning in life's uncertainty.

In the editorial-free spaces of the internet, human writing unfolds as a creative process. A unique creation beyond the confines of mere craftsmanship. People *like you and me*, whether bloggers or authors, understand that it is not the blind adherence to genre conventions that captivates others, but the right mix: it is the interplay between what we anticipate and what catches us off guard that truly holds us captive.

For many, this new space is a breeding ground for innovation, forging a deeper connection between storytelling and its audience. Others see it as a stage for influencers, fake news, and mass manipulation. With a bit of historical perspective, we have to state: We are all in the process of finding out.

Fact is: The enormous financial demands of producing traditional media — costs far from covered by the few coins spent at the newsstand — can no longer be sustained through a mixed calculation with advertising. The often-praised editorial work of the so-called "quality press" is losing its economic foundation.

"The good old target groups have had their day. They no longer offer reliable targets. Today's consumers behave more like schizophrenic, multiple personalities, showing increasingly little consistency and loyalty toward products and brands. Their consumption patterns are shaped by the experience of as many different moods and states as possible."

Translated from the original German text:

rheingold Institut Köln, "Das Ende der Zielgruppen?" 2005

Traditional target audiences, on which cultural creators long relied, no longer exist in their familiar form. Instead, we now see people who are constantly reinventing themselves, fragmented in both their identities and consumer behavior. Fragmented — shattered, broken apart? That would take us from thriller territory straight into splatter horror. So, what does this mean?

If we consider the diversity of roles we must navigate in modern life, we increasingly act — as one fitting quote puts it — like "multiple personalities, responding to brands and media in unpredictable and inconsistent ways." In a world where digital platforms keep people in a constant state of shifting moods, the lines between media creators and media consumers are also beginning to blur.

The internet provides us with both a space for creative exchange and a stage for conflict. Our communication — for our collective survival — is no less meaningful in the digital realm. If we learn to endure the contradictions of this new experience and shape them constructively, then democracy will remain strong — especially in an increasingly fragmented society.

If we accept the constant evolution of our own identity, the often unpredictable interactions online begin to feel "natural." This diversity can be challenging at times, but it also presents an opportunity to actively shape the public sphere.

Cloud infrastructures are fundamentally reshaping how and for whom we write. Once dismissed as mere entertainment or idle chatter, communication via smartphones and social media has long since entered the political arena. The moment a U.S. president used his phone — bypassing all diplomatic protocol — to arrange a meeting with a notoriously reclusive dictator, even academic elites could no longer afford to marginalize internet communication.

Whether social media is a waste of time or not, events like these highlight just how deeply digital structures have infiltrated public and political life. What was once dismissed as trivial is now woven into global discourse, with the power to shift geopolitical dynamics. The ability to write — and to respond appropriately — goes far beyond simply mastering the art of the emoji.

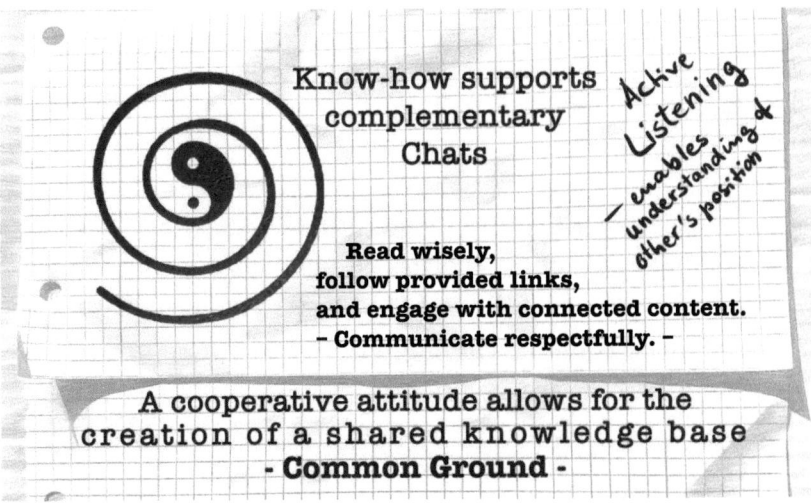

Know-how supports complementary Chats

Active Listening enables & understanding other's position

Read wisely, follow provided links, and engage with connected content.
- Communicate respectfully. -

A cooperative attitude allows for the creation of a shared knowledge base
- Common Ground -

Democracies that prioritize the individual over the state and embrace diversity must be able to demonstrate, especially in public spaces like the internet, how to navigate and sustain that diversity. More than that, they must show how this shared space can be made engaging and valuable through constructive contributions. That responsibility falls on all of us! What Hitchcock achieved with his camera's focus, we can all accomplish — whether in a chat thread or a comment — through *framing*.

With the know-how to place something in the right focus — framing, as it is — we can highlight aspects that matter to us, shaping how they are received by others through word choice and emphasis. At the same time, active listening helps us grasp the perspective from which our conversation partner approaches the topic.

The authors of *Efficient Communication* describe how we can deliberately and purposefully convey content to foster productive discussions. A key part of this is continuously establishing *common ground* — a shared foundation of mutually accepted assumptions and goals. Everyone knows the saying, "one word led to another ..." — a phrase that suggests being trapped in an exchange. But in communication, we are not passive victims; we are active participants, shaping the flow of conversation with every statement and response.

> *"When thinking in spirals, one does not see the communication partner as an opponent, nor is the goal to constantly refute the other's views. Instead, the focus is on developing a new, innovative line of thought to solve a problem."*
>
> Translated from the original German text:
>
> Ant / Nimmerfroh / Reinhard, "Effiziente Kommunikation," 2013, p. 123

By regularly engaging in fair and open discourse, we learn to frame discussions both consciously and for ourselves — to take an active role in shaping the narratives we engage with.

For every human being, it is crucial to learn how to engage with framing constructively in order to break free from the mind hijackers of our times.

When we recognize one-sided arguments that distort the balance of facts, it is up to us: Do we allow ourselves to be swept along in unison, or do we choose to trace the inconsistencies?

The open, unfiltered discourse space of the *internet* denies us the ability to choose whose opinions we encounter or who gets to impose their views on us. In the digital realm, this has led to the rise of >groups<, whose analog predecessors can be found in reading circles, social clubs, and regulars' tables at pubs. These groups provide their members with a limited exchange of ideas and information, typically built around shared interests, values, or political beliefs. However, these self-selected echo chambers ultimately restrict us, continuously reinforcing the same perspectives rather than exposing us to new ones. Online, such *bubbles* amplify pre-existing views to the point where education and reflection gradually fall by the wayside.

The classic W-questions can serve as our guide: Who is speaking? What is being said? When and where is the exchange taking place? Why do we respond the way we do? What is already known, and what is seeking change? This constant questioning helps us not only to gather information but also to grasp the deeper layers of communication.

We need *the words of the many* to reach a true understanding of what is meant — to find new solutions and to recognize the essential behind the sheer flood of facts.

If I'm asked about the most significant thing I've ever written, one comma and six words come to mind. The consultation process for this legal amendment, with all its pauses, consumed a year and a half and an unfathomable amount of paperwork. And even after that, it took several more years to gather the parliamentary approval that our laws demand. But having written something that would go on to affect the lives of hundreds of thousands of people instilled in me, well into adulthood, a profound reverence for writing — for the way it carries our thoughts and wishes forward through time.

It probably won't surprise you to hear that I've visited Herrenchiemsee twice already to see the permanent exhibition on the Constitutional Convention — the very place where, 75 years ago, the catalog of fundamental rights for our German Basic Law was drafted. Set in a former royal palace on a small island in Bavaria, this convention was a key moment in post-war history, where representatives from Germany's federal states came together to shape a democratic framework for a country still reeling from the devastation of World War II. If you ever find yourself deeply frustrated with the state of politics, I highly recommend the trip. Or, to borrow the words of a dear colleague — one who, sadly, is no longer with us: "Tell me, Ms. Ansén, why do you think we do politics? Because we can!"

For him, the idea of living a life without politics was simply unthinkable. He had witnessed firsthand the horrors that misguided politics could inflict upon people — politics that had failed catastrophically. Choosing not to take responsibility was never an option for him. Today, we live in far more stable times, and it is thanks to his generations who accepted personal sacrifices to secure the collective survival and the freedoms we now take for granted.

"Politics? Ugh! I want nothing to do with such a dirty business."

Please, believe me — I've heard this phrase more times than I can count. But the truth is, we have all become the civil servants of our own lives, managing responsibilities that shape not just our personal world but the society we live in. And especially in a democracy, no one should be under the illusion that they can simply step aside and opt out. Because democracy is more than the sum of its parts. A democracy worthy of its name thrives on mutual respect, diversity, and participation.

"Politics itself isn't really the problem," say many who deal with it professionally. "It's all these people!"

The line between opportunity and chaos is razor-thin. In reality, whenever large groups of people come together, it helps — immensely — to have writing. To put agreements and rules into words. To document the process of building consensus. Just as we have done since the very beginning of humankind!

In my eight years of volunteer work for our democracy, I've accumulated over twenty binders full of paperwork.

Serving my local community added another ten, and just school committees and booster clubs alone have filled up four more.

Our democratic processes seem to be populated by people who write. Cloud-based systems like *Confluence* promise relief, yet every few years, the inevitable system migration — where we selectively leave behind digital clutter — makes us regard our own filing cabinets with mixed feelings. The ten-year retention period underscores our right to be forgotten. But how does this shape our awareness of processes? Of democracy itself?

In Washington, back in 2014, I noticed an inscription in the visitor center waiting area of the Capitol — engraved in massive letters on the wall: *Consideration – consideration – consideration.*

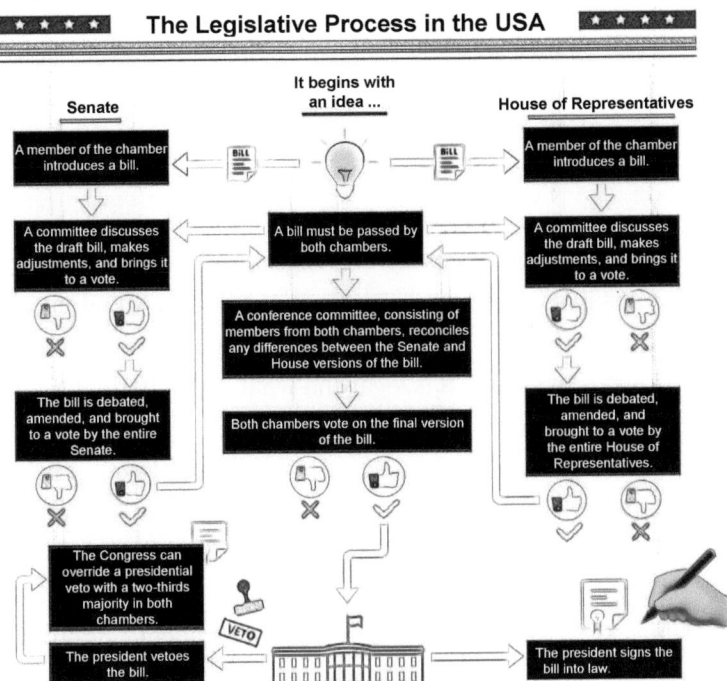

★ ★ ★ ★ **The Legislative Process in the USA** ★ ★ ★ ★

It begins with an idea ...

Senate

A member of the chamber introduces a bill.

A committee discusses the draft bill, makes adjustments, and brings it to a vote.

The bill is debated, amended, and brought to a vote by the entire Senate.

The Congress can override a presidential veto with a two-thirds majority in both chambers.

The president vetoes the bill.

A bill must be passed by both chambers.

A conference committee, consisting of members from both chambers, reconciles any differences between the Senate and House versions of the bill.

Both chambers vote on the final version of the bill.

VETO

House of Representatives

A member of the chamber introduces a bill.

A committee discusses the draft bill, makes adjustments, and brings it to a vote.

The bill is debated, amended, and brought to a vote by the entire House of Representatives.

The president signs the bill into law.

https://de.statista.com/infografik/16021/der-gesetzgebungsprozess-in-den-usa/

The guide proudly assured us how much value was placed on the lengthy deliberation process for every single law. After all, the people across fifty states had to stand behind its content. In a vast country like the United States, where *law enforcement* becomes increasingly difficult depending on population density, the internal conviction that laws apply to everyone is of paramount importance.

NO TEXTING WHILE DRIVING

IT'S THE LAW

It is no coincidence that you often hear and read the phrase:

"It's the law!"

These four words serve as a firm reminder that certain rules and regulations are not mere suggestions but legally binding requirements. You'll often find them on stickers in public places, on signs, or on products — highlighting specific laws related to safety regulations, speed limits, or health requirements.

Different parliaments handle written agreements and regulations in very different ways.

While Germany continues to expand its body of laws, other countries deliberately choose not to formalize many regulations into legal texts. In fact, cultural differences in this regard are significant. Italy, for example, has five times as many laws as the United Kingdom.

Everywhere, lawyers, notaries, and often a great deal of patience are required just to grasp what is legal and what is not. In the process, the sense of justice sometimes gets lost.

Germany's legislative process, which can be completed in just a few weeks, is designed to ensure the government remains capable of action. The result? Over 1,700 federal laws, containing more than 50,000 paragraphs, plus nearly 2,800 regulations — with numbers still rising. And that's before we even get to the laws of our sixteen federal states. Phew!

During a commemorative event marking "*70 Years of German Grundgesetz*" in the German Bundestag, the grandson of Theodor Heuss read from his notes: "The Basic Law must be clear and concise ... mindful of people's feelings."

It seems that in democratic processes, it's not just about what we agree on, but also how we put it into writing. Germany's democracy has long outgrown its youthful innocence and immediacy. Tied to a sprawling bureaucratic apparatus, modern democracies often appear to people as lumbering behemoths, slow, time-consuming, and ill-equipped to tackle the challenges of today and tomorrow.

Yet, during the last global crisis — the COVID-19 pandemic — democratically governed nations that emphasized personal responsibility and civic engagement generally fared better. For all the justified doubts, democracy in 2024 is still better than its reputation suggests!

Thinking, speaking up, and getting involved is not just rewarding —
it leads to better outcomes.

Looking at the economic growth and the remarkable improvement in
living conditions across the Baltic states over the past thirty years, it
becomes clear why neighboring, outdated autocracies feel unsettled.
Today, images and messages travel the globe without restriction.
And so, young people seeking opportunities for themselves and their
children are moving to Europe. Migration is no modern phenomenon,
but increased mobility tears families apart and uproots traditions.
We are in the midst of figuring out and shaping this new way of living
together.

More than ten years ago, the Irish government decided that
in a country so rich in tradition, it should not rely solely on a
narrow parliamentary majority to pass new laws or review
existing legislation. Instead, it organized a grassroots democratic
Constitutional Convention.

Among the pressing socio-political issues of the time were the
reduction of the presidential term, lowering the voting age to 16,
reforming the Dáil electoral system, removing blasphemy as
a criminal offense from the constitution, promoting women's
participation in public life, ensuring gender equality in the
constitution — and, of course, "marriage for all."

Citizens from all walks of life and politicians were invited to develop
new proposals for the Irish constitution, long known for its deep
Catholic traditions. This created a safe framework for one of Ireland's
most exciting — perhaps even boldest — democratic experiments to
date. And who took part in these discussions? Ordinary citizens from
across society ranging from a 20-year-old student to a retiree from a
small village.

This deliberation process stretched over three years — filled with discussions, debates, and an overwhelming amount of paperwork. Just as it always is when many perspectives collide.

When it came to marriage equality, two opposing main positions emerged: Supporters argued that marriage equality was not just a fundamental right but also a step toward greater equality in Irish society. Why should same-sex couples have fewer rights? It was not about special privileges but about equal rights for everyone. This stance was backed by numerous public figures and politicians advocating for a more inclusive society. Opponents feared that same-sex marriage would undermine traditional values, believing only man-woman marriage could sustain family and society.

During Ireland's deliberations on marriage equality, participants' views shifted noticeably. At the outset, many were uncertain or skeptical about the idea. However, over the course of years of in-depth discussions, numerous participants changed their stance.

Polls revealed that those who took part in the citizens' assembly or were well-informed were more likely to vote "Yes." Above all, it was the rational, fact-based discussions. The open debates, expert hearings, and carefully presented arguments that had a profound impact on people's views.

What made this referendum especially remarkable was Ireland's strong Catholic heritage. Homosexuality had only been decriminalized in 1993, making the shift in public opinion all the more striking. In fact, Ireland became the first country in the world to legalize same-sex marriage by popular vote — a decision that captured international attention. The process demonstrated something crucial: when people engage in open, structured dialogue, even deeply ingrained beliefs can evolve. In an era of increasing political division, this remains a powerful lesson.

The deliberation process within the citizens' assembly demonstrated how in-depth debates and discussions on equal footing can play a crucial role in shaping public opinion. In fact, in 2013, the assembly voted by an overwhelming majority of nearly 80% to recommend amending the Constitution to allow same-sex marriage. Ireland was ready for a major change. This recommendation was then put before the Irish people. After many more sessions and public debates, the referendum finally took place in 2015. The entire nation had its say: With 62% voting in favor, the majority of Irish citizens declared: Yes, we want *marriage equality*! A resounding message, one that would permanently reshape both the country and its legal framework.

No overnight success! Public awareness campaigns, emotional testimonies, and a flood of conversations on social media created the necessary environment for this shift to happen. But above all, it proved one thing: Change is possible — when we engage with one another!

Collaborative writing, especially when it comes to something as complex as a consensus paper, presents numerous challenges. These difficulties often lie in coordination, communication, and aligning content among the involved authors. Running into conflicts is only natural.

The question remains: How do we handle it?

If you've never experienced it yourself, you can hardly imagine how fiercely people — despite their shared desire for agreement — can argue over the final, "correct" wording. After a long process in which I failed to mediate between two opposing positions, I took a pen and scribbled a note: > Humans matter more than words! <

That note has hung above my desk ever since as a constant reminder. Because as one of the authors involved, I had come to realize that the people who dedicate themselves to these processes will be the very same ones we need to collaborate with on future solutions.

How can we successfully collaborate on documents with many contributors?

Perhaps you've heard this classic remark in a meeting before: > Everything has already been said — just not by everyone yet! < To prevent such situations, a well-structured session with strong moderation can make all the difference. The goal is always to establish *common ground.*

By actively steering discussions toward fresh, constructive contributions and minimizing repetition, we can keep conversations more focused — and ultimately, more productive.

Just like reading, an engaged and mindful discussion can shift our awareness — leaving us feeling enriched and alive.

This is exactly how we should approach writing meeting minutes: On the one hand, to give those who weren't present the opportunity to participate; on the other, to challenge ourselves to take complex, multidimensional thoughts and distill them into a linear sequence of letters. Preferably into clear, tangible words!

The ability to apply linguistic compression pays off once again, especially if one aims to avoid producing lifeless, tedious documents fit only for hole-punching and filing.

Meetings can be exhausting, especially when we focus on active listening to absorb all the details and nuances of a discussion. Active listening demands constant attention, making it both mentally and emotionally taxing. It requires us not only to understand words but also to read between the lines, observe body language, and interpret the emotions and perspectives of others.

Breaks are essential!

Despite all the technical tools available today, taking handwritten notes remains a crucial skill for capturing ideas, opinions, and decisions. In the whirlwind of spoken words, these inputs can quickly blend with our own thoughts, sparking new ideas. While that is not necessarily a bad thing, it can cause some participants to drift so far off track that following the original thread becomes a challenge. This is precisely why parliamentary sessions are still transcribed word for word. Public portions of these sessions remain accessible for anyone interested — now or in future.

Deep-seated disagreements, fixation on details, and emotionally charged arguments can sometimes make us doubt whether we're still addressing the core of a problem. When that happens, I remind myself:

Embrace every contradiction — it sharpens your thinking.

Redirecting and reframing — techniques that work wonders in parenting — are just as effective among adults. A brief shift to the meta-level can help break free from the nitty-gritty, allowing everyone to refocus on the bigger picture and shared goals.

Challenges	Solution Approach
Documenting diversity of opinions	Different perspectives are often lost when dissenting opinions are smoothed out. A conscious effort to document all viewpoints is needed to provide a complete picture of the discussion.
Process orientation instead of just final results	Decisions are often recorded without capturing the steps and discussions that led to them. Documenting the course of discussions makes future reviews and adjustments easier.
Valuing dissenting opinions	Disagreements are often seen as obstacles rather than valuable contributions. Respectfully documenting these perspectives helps identify blind spots and develop more robust solutions.
Clear responsibilities & feedback loops	Without clear responsibilities and feedback mechanisms, misunderstandings and delays can occur. Regular feedback rounds and designated responsibilities ensure smooth processes.
Structured, clear protocols	Meeting minutes are often either too vague or overly detailed. A clear structure of key points, opinions, and decisions improves clarity and allows for quick reference.
Using protocols as dynamic tools	Meeting minutes are often viewed as static documents that lose relevance after the session. Instead, they should serve as a living reference for future discussions and decisions.

Writing is not just a craft but an act of responsibility, one that enables us to shape our societies. Yet, as individuals within the whole, we are more a medium that happens to hold a pen than solitary originators of ideas. We fish from the collective stream of thoughts, selecting what seems useful, and present it in a way that inspires others to think further. In the rarest cases do we write something meant to last forever. And even then, it is but fragments — never book's worth.

It is remarkable how the smallest details can spark the biggest debates. These moments reveal the true challenges of collaborative writing — not the proper use of words, but the people behind them, with their beliefs and convictions, making the process so complex.

Yet, if we remember that

"Humans matter more than words,"

we can find solutions that are built to last. At the end of the day, what truly matters is our ability to reach out to one another and to preserve the capacity to keep writing — together.

Writing is far more than just a tool for recording thoughts — it is our most powerful means of shaping shared ideas.

Especially in a democracy, the conversations and compromises behind every formulation are the most crucial part of the process. Not every detail is critical, but the exchange itself sharpens our thinking and deepens our understanding of different perspectives. If we keep this in mind, even the most challenging meetings can be productive and meaningful — because in the end, it is not just about the words on the page, but about how we arrived at them together.

The idea that all writing in the future will be handled by eager AI-powered writing assistants is a rather one-sided promise of salvation. Sure, with 50–100 characters per second, they can be a helpful relief in many situations. But the real challenge isn't finding someone — or something — to write for us. It is about bringing people together to think about what should be written in the first place.

Politics was, is, and always will be a team sport — one in which full-time officials and volunteers work hand in hand to shape public space and democratic processes. The collaboration between these two groups is indispensable for social cohesion and the ongoing development of our society.

The Irish Constitutional Convention, which led to the recommendation for *marriage equality*, serves as a more recent example of how powerful democratic discourse can be. We do not always have to look back solely at distant debates — those of the Roman Senate, the French National Assembly, the founding of the League of Nations, or the closed-door sessions at Herrenchiemsee — though thanks to their recorded words, we certainly can.

In Ireland, people from diverse backgrounds in our time were brought together to discuss and ultimately prepare a decision that would change an entire nation. It was not just about amending a single paragraph in the constitution — it was about fostering a dialogue that took all perspectives into account.

Writing and collective decision-making require more than just ink on paper — they demand listening, understanding, and the willingness to work together toward solutions.

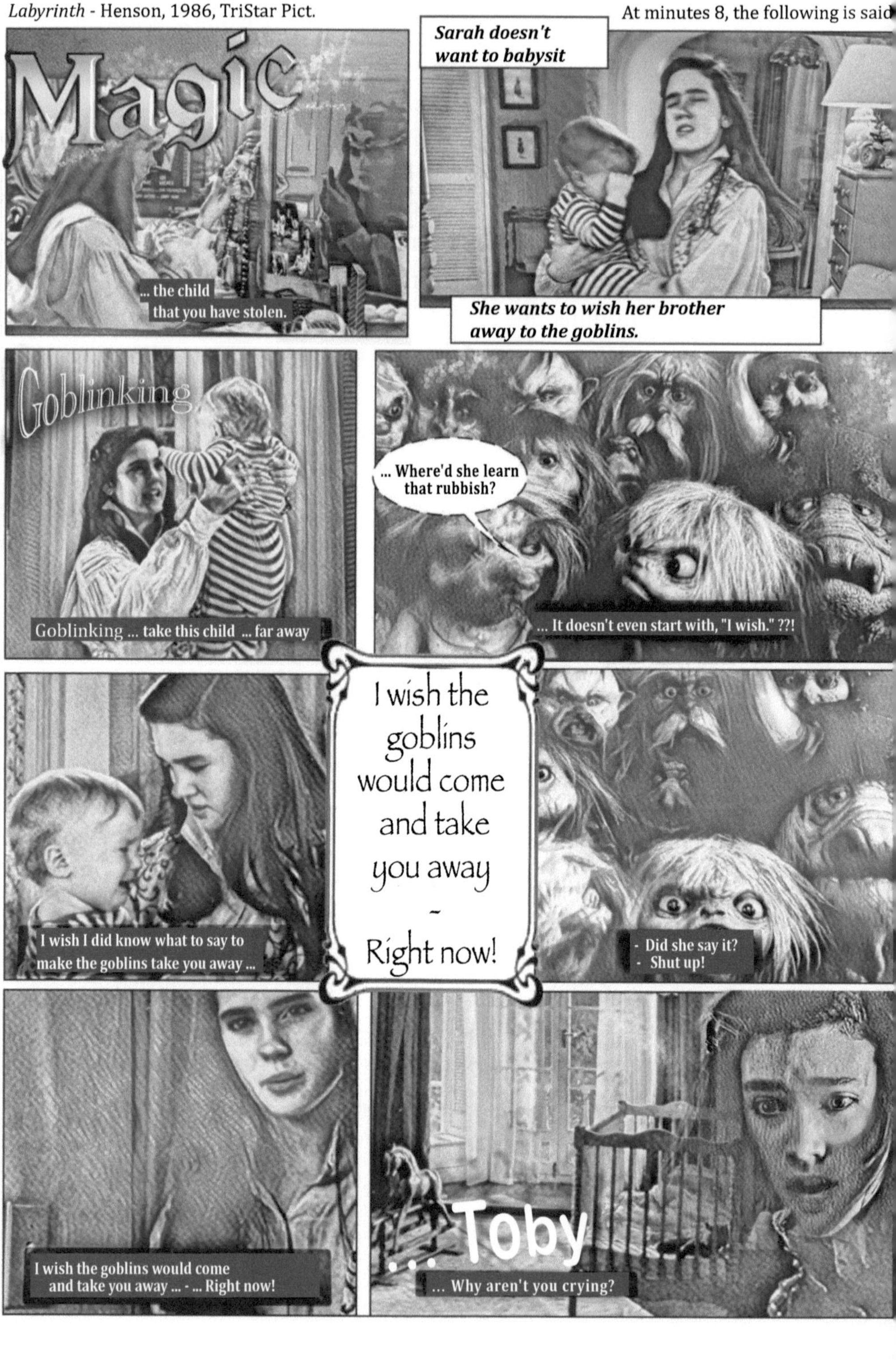

Today, we no longer manage the world's knowledge alone. Artificial intelligence (AI) has stepped in to assist us, promising to ease some of our burdens. But how do we bring this magic to life? How do we set these language models into motion and make them work for us? The precision of our words determines whether we receive the help we seek or end up frustrated by a lack of cooperation. Not such a new challenge after all, is it?

Sigmund Freud already described the fascination of language as an "original magic." For early humans, language was the medium through which reality was shaped — a way to make the mystical tangible and to influence the world through words.

Let's take a moment to imagine how astonishing it must have been for early humans when the first of our ancestors began to form words and concepts. Archaeological discoveries, such as Acheulean hand axes found in Africa, suggest that as early as 1.76 million years ago, some of our predecessors possessed the cognitive abilities necessary to craft such complex tools. These tools were not mere improvisations; their reproduction required precise planning, multi-step techniques, and the sharing of knowledge within a community.

Without some form of language — or at least symbolic communication — it is difficult to imagine how this knowledge could have been passed down. As know-how improved human life, so grew the awareness that innovation and tradition must converge — deliberately and with purpose.

Steve de Shazer, in his exploration of the early days of psychotherapy, much like Mike Mandl, examines how mere thoughts shape our language and how, through conscious application, we can shift *'from problem talk to solution talk.'*

Language has always been with us in its finest nuances — like a form of magic, it transforms, inspires, and opens new possibilities. The importance of *speaking the right words* is a lesson woven into vast fairy tales, carried forward all the way into modern times.

Playfully, we learn just how crucial the precise use of language and the correct recall of details can be. Whether I wish to transform back from a stork to a caliph, escape the robbers' cave as *Ali Baba*, trust that my table will set itself with a feast, or hope the magic cudgel will come to my aid — a misremembered  spell can lead to disaster.

Goethe's *The Sorcerer's Apprentice* reminds us of this, a lesson made unforgettable by Walt Disney's *Fantasia*, where *Mickey Mouse* takes on the role of the overconfident apprentice.

"Speak the right words!" — this wisdom applies just as much to our use of language in the digital world.

Every training session on AI usage promotes the magic of the right "prompts" — those inputs that guide language models like ChatGPT. Just as in fairy tales, finding the right words can lead to profound changes in our world. To overcome speechlessness, I dedicate an entire chapter to this crucial topic of the future.

The responsibility of equipping future generations with digital media literacy is immense.

Those who care about *education for all* would do well to introduce as many people as possible, as quickly as possible, to the interactive process of using AI. Learning, interactive, as many as possible?

That means actively integrating the topic into school education? Exactly.

Students should grasp the fundamental concepts behind machine learning, algorithms, and data processing. This can be introduced in a playful manner — through programming simple AI applications or engaging with interactive examples. So far, so familiar; the demand itself is nothing new.

But language models like ChatGPT? How is everyone supposed to learn how to write? Just as in the time of Socrates — when the use of writing was fiercely debated as a *revolution* for accessible education — we now find ourselves once again at a threshold in human history, hesitating.

Our working world will undergo immense changes in the coming years, and we carry a responsibility toward all future generations. Once again, we face the challenge of evolving as a learning organization — humanity itself — and contributing to the creation of meaning.

To meet this challenge, it is crucial that children engage in shared learning experiences, exploring questions such as: How does AI impact our privacy, job markets, and social justice?

Language models like ChatGPT have the potential to provide every single student with individualized support, catering specifically to their questions and needs. They offer explanations and examples, adjust difficulty levels dynamically, and accommodate different learning styles. No missed lessons, learning happens anytime, anywhere curiosity strikes.

In a democratic society built on inclusion and diversity, access to key cultural skills must be available to all. When used correctly, ChatGPT and other AI tools can enhance our command of language — teaching us to use words strategically while also questioning them in the process.

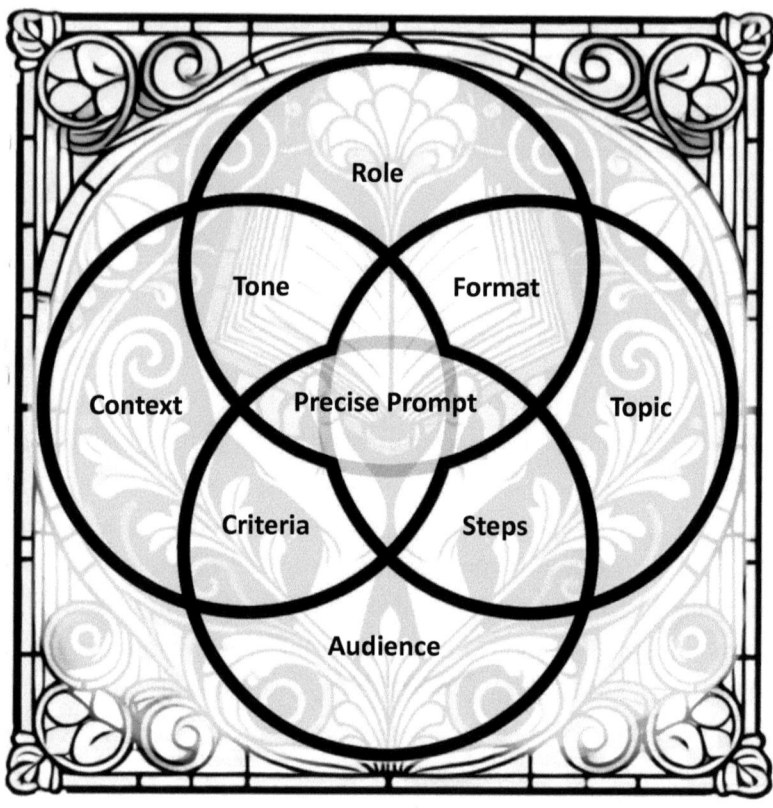

If you are someone who has deliberately avoided AI applications until now, you will find a step-by-step guide in the appendix to help you gain your own experience.

Unsurprisingly, in the showcase above, apart from the word "Prompt," you won't find any terms that we haven't already explored in the previous pages.

Whether it is participation in democratic processes or engagement in digital development: Knowing the right words and commands allows us to express ourselves, share our opinions, and contribute to collective decision-making — again and again!

Democratic societies rely on their citizens' ability to make informed decisions and keep discussions alive. Engaging with AI through tools like ChatGPT once again challenges us to think critically, grasp complex interconnections, and actively participate in our communities. Our daily lives already benefit from speech recognition, image processing, and personalized platforms. A language model like ChatGPT can serve as a patient and respectful tutor, adapting to each user's needs. Learning — wherever I am, whenever my curiosity takes me further.

To achieve this, I need to tell the language model — in writing or verbally — what role it should take on when interacting with me. Should ChatGPT act as a tutor, a coach, or an expert? This choice influences how it responds and what type of information or guidance it provides. Equally important is expressing my expectations for the response: Do I want an essay, a short list, a dialogue, or an in-depth analysis? By specifying the format clearly, I determine the structure of the result.

At the same time, I must also define how I want to receive the response: should it be formal, objective, or humorous? The tone of the answer ensures that it aligns with the context I have in mind. To get the most relevant and useful output, my questions should be tied directly to a specific topic and framed within a clear context, ensuring that the suggested steps match my criteria.

Only I know the target audience I have in mind when engaging in a conversation with ChatGPT. If I keep all of this in mind, I will most often receive a response on the first attempt that has the depth I need to take the next step in my thinking.

Just like good writing: The art of prompting is less about magic and more about precision. The clearer and more intentional our question, the more likely we are to receive a focused and relevant answer.

A language model like ChatGPT generates responses by calculating probabilities, using so-called *tokens* — word fragments or entire words that are sequentially assembled into an answer. Each token is selected based on the likelihood of following the previous words or tokens. To mistake this probabilistic process for magic would be misleading, as it is a mathematically defined mechanism, not an act of sorcery. While this AI essentially "predicts" which word is likely to come next, its responses are built on patterns and probabilities — not on creative or mystical thought.

The longer people choose to ignore the opportunities of equitably used AI, the more room we give to myths — some portraying it as a miraculous breakthrough, others dismissing it as an overhyped gimmick. These extremes thrive in the absence of real understanding, shaping public perception instead of informed experience. But as with all turning points in history, progress is neither magic nor accident. Ultimately, we still define the context.

Historical spells have been a part of human storytelling and rituals for centuries. In many cultures, these incantations were believed to be mystical formulas that would only work if spoken correctly. Often written in ancient languages or dialects, they carried an added aura of secret knowledge and power. These magical phrases were meant to influence natural forces, provide protection, or unlock hidden doors — whether to knowledge or supernatural realms.
If we draw this historical arc into the present, we can see a similar dynamic in our interaction with artificial intelligence. For decades, the prevailing narrative insisted that everyone would need to learn programming. Instead, resourceful people taught AI how to code — and now, all we truly need for the future is our language!

The ability to understand AI and communicate with it effectively determines whether we can harness its full potential or whether it remains *silent* to us. The elixir of our time lies in recognizing that language — both then and now — is more than mere information; it is the key to power and transformation.

And sometimes, speed is of the essence! For the challenges of our ever more crowded world, we do not have another few million years to spare. No matter how educated or well-read I may be, a conversation with ChatGPT quickly reveals what I (still) don't know — and which aspects are truly valuable for my decision-making.

The dynamic between individual knowledge and collective intelligence is paving the way for a new kind of learning. ChatGPT weaves together the writings of people who, across continents and generations, have shared their thoughts with the world. True "deep learning" emerges when human participation not only absorbs the world's existing knowledge but continuously expands and refines it. This process is shaping a kind of "global library," one that both preserves and evolves knowledge simultaneously. In the future, we will build and access knowledge at unprecedented speed. Transgenerational learning, once confined to oral and written traditions within smaller communities, has entered a new era — driven by AI and global exchange.

This new form of learning culture will be crucial in tackling the challenges of our time with the speed and depth required by life in an increasingly global and complex world. After all, for our collective survival, we once again need new solutions!

Our thoughts, whether conscious or unconscious, are always in motion, making it difficult to capture and put them down on paper.
As long as we live, everything is in flux and subject to constant change — not just our thoughts, but also our metabolism. Within our neural pathways, information is continuously transmitted back and forth. What we feel shapes what we think, what we do and say, and, of course, what we write.
Heraclitus captured these observations in two simple words: *panta rhei* — "everything flows."

We cannot step into the same river twice. The current of life that surrounds us is ever-renewing, always carrying fresh waters. Capturing thoughts — even just on a scrap of paper, a brief note, or in a few well-chosen words — is no small task, for in doing so, we resist the very nature of constant change.
And yet, we do it — because we can. Because we have learned that a single good idea can move mountains and benefit others — at best, even supporting our collective survival. We live through and by exchanging with others; to be connected is the fabric we are made of, we are, at our core, social beings.
If I scribble a little ink onto paper, I can be satisfied — even without having written a book. Because everything we write, we write with intention, in this moment of pause, ideally, with joy. We shape contexts, selecting from the vast array of sounds and syllables what seems most useful in this fleeting moment in time. Artificial intelligence and digital tools may help us organize, but the act of capturing and creating remains, at its core, profoundly human. That's exactly the aspect we're focusing on in this final chapter.

If we recognize that human development — indeed, life itself — is an ongoing, ever-evolving process, then we must also acknowledge that our language never comes to rest.

With his extensive work on morphology, Goethe laid out a structure to help us understand the recognizable patterns of change in life cycles. If we examine the evolution of "marriage" over the past four generations, we inevitably stumble upon the fact that our legal and social contexts have shifted dramatically — swinging back and forth like a pendulum.

In the early 20th century, marriage was viewed almost exclusively as a heterosexual, religious institution aimed at procreation and creating economic and social alliances. Through the 1950s and 1960s, it remained deeply patriarchal in many countries, with women lacking independent rights. It was not until 1958 that Germany abolished the so-called "right of obedience" for husbands, which had granted them legal authority over their wives. And not until 1977 could women work without their husband's permission. In those days, the idea of "marriage for all" would have sounded more like a call for servitude than one for emancipation.

The very question of whether monogamy was truly *natural* had entered public discourse. With the women's rights and equality movements of the 1960s, marriage began to evolve into a partnership between equals. Couples could now divorce more easily without facing complete social ostracization. Love and emotional connection became increasingly important for those seeking commitment — turning into the ultimate measure of a relationship's worth.

Liz Taylor married eight times.

The liberalization of divorce laws led to a significant rise in divorce rates across many Western countries. Living together without the formal vow of marriage became a widely accepted alternative.

In 2001, the Netherlands became the first country to legalize same-sex marriage. Today, marriage is increasingly seen as a partnership of equals. A dynamic evolution that continues to reshape cultural and societal norms, as well as traditional gender roles.

However, in some parts of the world, the traditional concept of marriage remains firmly in place, rooted in the belief that gender roles are dictated by nature or divine will. In these societies, the patriarchal leadership of men is taken for granted, just as the domestic role of women is seen as self-evident.

So if we find ourselves at a bus stop with a random group of people — of different backgrounds and ages — and someone mentions the idea of "being married off" or simply says "marriage," a multitude of associations will be triggered in each person's mind, shaped by contexts we may not even fully be aware of.

Wilhelm Salber applied Goethe's morphological approach to psychology by examining the shifting meanings within both individual experiences and broader society. He did not merely study how terms and images evolve over time but also how they generate new meanings and ideas within us. Every use of a term carries with it a multitude of additional meanings and interpretations, shaped by the interplay of culture, zeitgeist, and personal experience. This dynamic influences us both consciously and unconsciously in our daily lives, shaping the reality we construct.

Looking at the modern diversity of interpretations of marriage, we see morphological logic in action: Marriage is not a fixed concept but a living, evolving idea whose context we continuously experience anew. Or, as the Irish so beautifully put it:

"Marriage is a sealed letter that we only open at sea."

From David Hume to Wilhelm Salber to Steven Pinker, one thing becomes clear: The most important words we use — by far — are verbs. They are much more than mere instructions for action or descriptions of states; they shape our entire understanding of the world. Hume illustrates this through the structure of the Latin terms: *esse* (to be), *nosse* (to know), and *velle* (to will). These terms do not merely represent static states but reflect the fundamental tensions of experience, perception, and action — tensions that shape our grasp of reality itself: What we do!

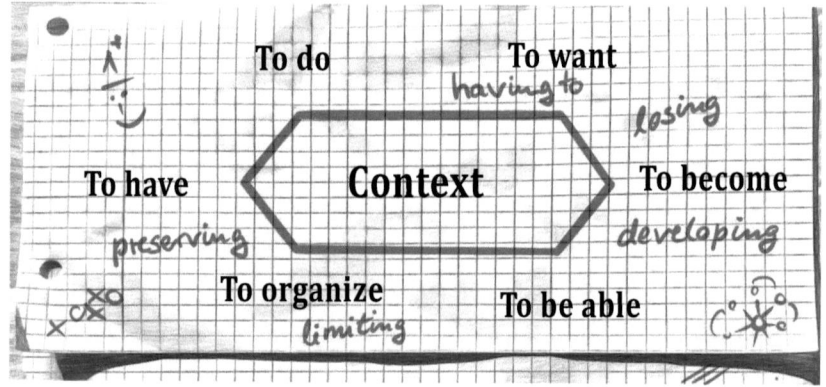

What seems contradictory and illogical at first glance is, in the organic fabric of our humanity, deeply interconnected. If we truly want to decipher the workings of our consciousness — the so-called *sixth dimension* — we must brace ourselves for a kind of mental acrobatics that is not to everyone's taste.

Bringing the conflicting needs and impressions of our lives into harmony challenges us day by day. As humankind, as a learning organization, we live out an invisible *generational contract* — a division of labor shaped by the interplay between species preservation and the drive for innovation.

Will AI models soon write the better books? Perhaps.

Regardless of the medium, true understanding requires communication and exchange — through conversation, with children, within families, and in partnerships. Because exchange means peace, and our world needs peace to survive.

Even though the world's knowledge is now growing exponentially, it is still humans who remain the ultimate guarantors of interpreting knowledge and making value judgments. Without other people, it becomes difficult to grasp the meaning behind information and to use it in context.

Innovation research shows that true breakthroughs often emerge where people encounter different perspectives and open themselves to new ways of seeing.

There are people who believe they know me without ever having read a single line I've written. It may well be that this was the very reason why my German teacher insisted on making me read every essay aloud in front of the class — but did it really create more understanding? As far as I recall, quite the opposite.

Forcing someone to pay attention rarely pays off — at least for a writer. If anything, we become even more critical when confronted with unexpected thoughts from others, instinctively searching for flaws. Sometimes, a book simply sparks envy — something I had yet to learn as an adult. That's why the smug words of a longtime colleague stayed with me: "Oh, so you think you need to publish a book at thirty-six?" That hit me right after I had honestly shared my disappointment over a publisher's rejection.

Well, we don't always have to say out loud what we think. But writing is different: Whatever I put into words is inevitably the result of what I have thought. So for those who truly want to understand a person, it is always wise to look at the ink of their written words rather than judge them by the surface — shiny or not.

For our transgenerational learning to succeed, it is crucial not to cling rigidly to the past but to continuously reinterpret knowledge and values, strengthening the narratives that drive us forward.

By writing, we create our world, reflect on our actions, and set out together toward new horizons.

In a broader context, the growing trend toward *open access* supports this mindset: More and more scientific publications are being made freely available, fostering global knowledge exchange and collaboration. Projects in which researchers around the world share their data and insights accelerate our collective understanding and contribute to solving global challenges.

On a smaller scale, many feel liberated not only within their private circles but also in public — able to say, "I like him; he's a good one!" and leave a *Like* on social media. Or to warn others early on without splitting ears or cutting off fingers, as was once done to brand someone a fraud or a thief. Today, a simple comment or *Dislike* on a platform is enough to signal to a wide audience who deserves trust and who does not.

In the fast-paced digital world, the consequences of a lack of education weigh more heavily on us. There are more critical eyes, and a simple slip of the pen — or the keyboard — can have far-reaching effects when we get carried away in the heat of the moment. No longer excused, we just have "misspeak" or, rather, "miswrite."

El Hotze recently had to learn this lesson the hard way, risking his entire career over a careless remark about a botched assassination attempt on a politician. More than once, our moral compass has been shaped by a simple commandment: "Thou shalt not kill." A shame when one's inner needle is so hopelessly stuck.

A lack of empathy is not some childish affliction we naturally outgrow. It is a weakness that weighs on our society's progress.

We bear responsibility for what we write — always.

Whether it's "2 box Negro Kisses" on a shopping list, "You asshole" in an email, or simply "Die" in a chat — flanked by emojis or not. We really should pay attention to what we write. It stays.

At the very least, it immediately seeps into our collective consciousness — the home we should all feel safe in.

Our ability to move fluidly between concepts sometimes falters. Steven Pinker calls this the "special quirks" of human thought.

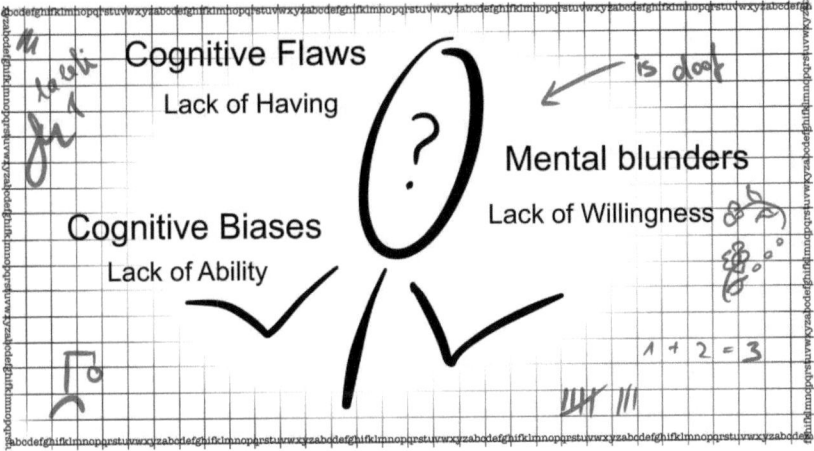

Indeed, sometimes it's worth flipping the switch in our minds and consciously engaging with the sixth dimension — deciding which linguistic and logical concepts we truly want to deepen.

Think first, then write — this is how our thoughts *manifest*.

If we trace the etymology of the word "manifest"—we study a word's true meaning — we come across its Latin roots: *manus* (hand) and *festus* (firm).

Meaning that our thoughts quite literally become *tangible by hand*.

For a long time, people have tried to decipher the supposedly *"grim"* German character — one man even felt compelled to cement his version of it in a book titled *Mein Kampf.*

But those with clear eyes and hearts already saw where such an ideology would lead. Still, many school dropouts and traumatized survivors of World War I saw in it a way out of poverty and injustice. Sadly, it was not the last case of collective failure in the long history of humankind.

Time and again, there are people who nourish similar hopes. Who tie human survival to the question of who should survive. Who believe they have the right to decide who, where, and how people are allowed to live.

In Iran, people whose parents' generation was still over 60% illiterate devoted themselves to a revolution — even as their own great scholars warned against it. As long as a small, educated minority can be silenced through house arrest, labor camps, or execution, societies remain vulnerable to tyranny and the self-enrichment of those in power.

The separation of powers and federalism, as introduced after World War II, can protect a community from excessive political ambition. But they can also make democracy so inefficient and unappealing that no one wants to participate anymore.

Education for all is not an all-inclusive package for prosperity, security, and peace. It is the beginning of a collective process of awareness — like learning together at the kitchen table, which can be the first step toward change.

Our ability to engage in exchange with one another, across time and place, is one of the most crucial building blocks for looking beyond our own horizon and discovering what is truly useful.

Many self-help books insist that we just need to let go in order to find salvation. That always sounds a bit suicidal to me — but maybe that's just because I'm not enlightened yet.

If everything flows — which, after all, is a core idea of meditation — does that mean we should simply *let go* of everything? Stop letting concepts into our consciousness? Just feel free and establish direct contact with the universe? And further: Should we just pack our elected representatives off to a meditation retreat and hope for the best? Would we even need parliaments anymore? And if not, who would administer us and ensure our survival?

Everything we have learned about human coexistence testifies to the necessity of taking responsibility and letting go of what no longer serves us.

We need values to guide us and we need the freedom to let go of outdated ideals when they no longer serve us. A parliament made up entirely of *"let-goers"* could easily drift into irrelevance. But one that recognizes when change is necessary contributes to collective growth. As Ireland has shown us: Living in a democracy challenges us. Education for all challenges us.

Our freedom to form opinions and act together not only moves us forward but also challenges us to actively set the course and constantly question ourselves.

Democracy thrives on renewal, and that overwhelms many of our fellow citizens.

No matter how much empathy we have for democracy as a historically young form of government, all democrats must acknowledge that in every country, a third of the population votes for conservative parties. It is a mandate for everything to please stay exactly as it never was. As it may have only felt beautiful, pure, and stable in our hearts without ever holding up to critical examination.

For history not to be, as Napoleon once joked, *the lie* we all agree upon, we need the voices of many.

For change to emerge in a way that benefits us all, we must develop an awareness of the so-called *status quo* — the present state of affairs, which is as impossible to hold onto as the center of a flowing river. The status quo is anything but a neutral point. Rather, it represents an intersection of perspectives and privileges that align with the spirit of the times and are all too often perceived as immovable.

The idea that we can just leave the writing to others — or better yet, to AI — fails to recognize the danger of solidifying that very intersection of ideas, beliefs, and implicit privileges hidden within the status quo, often suffocating critical questions.

A society that can embrace the change it needs thrives on the shared acts of writing, debating, and questioning the very ideas that shape it.

Writing and language are more than just functional tools — they are instruments of meaning-making. Human beings bring meaning into the world through their creativity, their ability to interpret, and their ethical reflections.

Humans should not unlearn the art of writing or fully delegate it to machines or political structures, as it is essential for our collective intellectual growth.

As is written in the Bible: "You are the salt of the earth." It is up to us to bring out what truly matters. Writing allows us to organize our thoughts, shape our identity, participate in democracy, and actively contribute to the formation of cultural and societal values.

Find something worth writing. Spark good thoughts. Keep the possibility of a happy ending firmly in sight. Do not leave writing to those who do not have our best interests at heart.

At the end of every book, I look at my many notes, and once again, not all of them found their way onto these pages.

"I did my best," I would tell the interrogating officer, followed by an anecdote from Edgar Wallace: A clever reporter once pressed him on why he did not revise his books more carefully. "The revision of my last book is my next book!" What may sound arrogant is something I have come to understand well in my fifties. The questions and narratives that move us stay with us for a lifetime.

Even if we must never take ourselves too seriously, refusing to take responsibility is not an option for a future worth living. Without our writing, democracy itself would slowly starve intellectually and be devoured from the edges.

Think along. Speak up. Get involved. And WRITE!

That's how we all stay alive!

*To spare you from the following brackets (m/f/d), please assume >ALL< when reading nouns, should there be any doubt.
After reading so many pages, you have likely realized why this text does not attempt to squeeze the world into a binary system of two genders.

I used to compile sources and links for you at this point, always introducing them with the remark:
Owing to the lightness of the text, it comes without footnotes — but not without deeper thought.
What followed was a list of sources, cited as we are accustomed to in academic contexts. It was always a lot of work and took time.

In 2024, I could simply ask an AI to analyze my text and generate a bibliography for me. Possible, but pointless!
So instead, I prefer to make use of your expectation that the appendix usually contains something useful — and surprise you:

To explore the topics mentioned in more depth, you will find a guide here on how CHATGPT by OPENAI can generate context based on given keywords in just seconds. A free option is available.

- After each session, CHATGPT forgets who asked what and patiently answers all your questions again the next time.

- All it takes is setting up an account on OPENAI's official website: https://chatgpt.com/auth/login. A phone number is required.

Be mindful:
There are many hybrid applications in so-called app stores that are ultimately just modified versions of the GPT model.

Once your account is registered, you are ready to go. Enjoy exploring!

Here is what your research could look like, depending on the language you use:

Was ist „Wie wir erzählen..." von Vera Ansén für eine Publikation?

„Wie wir erzählen..." ist eine wissenschaftliche Veröffentlichung von Vera Ansén, die sich mit narrativen Strukturen und Erzählweisen beschäftigt. In dieser Arbeit untersucht Ansén, wie Geschichten in verschiedenen Kontexten erzählt werden und welche erzählerischen Techniken dabei zum Einsatz kommen. Der Fokus liegt dabei auf den Methoden und Mechanismen, die das Erzählen von Geschichten prägen, und darauf, wie diese von den Rezipienten wahrgenommen und interpretiert werden.

And further...

T2 - Trainspotting?

The term "T2: Trainspotting" refers to the 2017 British film that serves as a sequel to the iconic 1996 film *Trainspotting*, directed by Danny Boyle. Both films are based on the works of Scottish author Irvine Welsh, with the first movie adapting his novel *Trainspotting* and the sequel drawing elements from his follow-up novel *Porno*, among other sources.

Trainspotting (1996):

- **Plot:** The original *Trainspotting* film is set in Edinburgh, Scotland, and follows a group of heroin addicts, particularly focusing on Mark Renton (played by Ewan McGregor), as they navigate the highs and lows of addiction, friendship, and the grim realities of life in a depressed urban setting. The film is known for its dark humor, energetic direction, and stark portrayal of addiction.
- **Cultural Impact:** The film became a cultural phenomenon, influencing a generation with its distinctive style, memorable soundtrack, and exploration of youth culture and addiction. It's often regarded as one of the greatest British films of all time.

Gib mir die Antwort kürzer und in Deutsch

T2: Trainspotting ist die Fortsetzung des Kultfilms *Trainspotting* von 1996, beide unter der Regie von Danny Boyle. Der erste Film handelt von einer Gruppe von Heroinabhängigen in Edinburgh und wurde für seinen Stil und seine Darstellung von Jugendkultur und Sucht gefeiert. T2 spielt 20 Jahre später und zeigt die Wiedervereinigung der Hauptfiguren, die sich mit dem Älterwerden, Reue und den Konsequenzen ihrer früheren Entscheidungen auseinandersetzen. Die Fortsetzung wurde für ihre nostalgische Stimmung und die Weiterentwicklung der Charaktere gelobt.

So, everything's easy then?

The GPT assistant seems to put just about any question into context somehow. So why the complaints like *"The smart get smarter, and the dumb get dumber"*? While compiling this appendix, I once again stumbled upon interesting details that I hadn't been fully aware of while writing.

The situation: Somewhere in my office (or one of the many places where I keep additional papers), there is a newspaper article in which I had once highlighted the quote: *"Democracy is the oligarchy of those who have time."*

So, I casually asked CHATGPT's CREATIVE WRITING COACH:

Creative Writing Coach ›

Wer titelte Demokratie ist die Oligarchie der Zeit habenden?

Der Titel „Demokratie ist die Oligarchie der Zeit habenden" stammt von dem deutschen Soziologen Paul Nolte. Er verwendete diesen Ausdruck, um darauf hinzuweisen, dass in einer modernen Demokratie diejenigen, die über mehr Zeit und Ressourcen verfügen, auch einen größeren Einfluss auf politische Prozesse haben. Nolte kritisiert damit die ungleiche Teilhabe und die damit verbundene Verzerrung demokratischer Ideale.

Wann schrieb Paul Nolte das?

Paul Nolte prägte den Ausdruck „Demokratie ist die Oligarchie der Zeit habenden" in einem Essay, der 2003 in der „Frankfurter Allgemeinen Zeitung" veröffentlicht wurde. Der Essay diskutiert die Ungleichheit in der politischen Partizipation und kritisiert, dass in der Demokratie vor allem diejenigen Einfluss haben, die über genügend Zeit und Ressourcen verfügen.

When I tried to reproduce the result with CHATGPT, this is what it looked like:

ChatGPT 4o ›

Wer titelte Demokratie ist die Oligarchie der Zeit habenden?

Der Titel "Demokratie ist die Oligarchie der Zeit habenden" stammt von **Karlheinz Deschner**, einem deutschen Schriftsteller und Religionskritiker. Er hat diesen Satz in seinem Buch „Der Moloch: Eine kritische Geschichte der USA" formuliert. Deschner wollte damit ausdrücken, dass in einer Demokratie vor allem diejenigen Einfluss nehmen, die die Zeit und die Ressourcen haben, sich politisch zu engagieren, während viele andere aufgrund von Zeitmangel, beispielsweise durch Arbeit, weniger Einfluss haben.

In terms of intellectual history, it makes sense — you just have to keep thinking.

So keep asking   ... this can go on forever ...

Space for Your Notes

Band I

Erkennbar, verständlich, wählbar
... zu MEHR gesellschaftlicher Mitwirkung!

mit Bonuskapitel 8

ISBN 978-3-759-71176-2

Erkennen Sie Ihre Talente und Wirkung, damit Sie sich selbstbewusst durch die Aufgaben bewegen, die uns das Leben vor die Füße spült!

Finden wir Klarheit in unseren Absichten, gefallen uns Rollen und teilen wir gerne Aufträge. Denn gut organisieren zu können, versichert uns immer interessanter Aufgaben.

Mit diesem Sachbuch fällt es Ihnen fortan leicht, ohne Angst vor andere Menschen zu treten. Einfach einladen: MACHEN WIR WAS!

Band II

Wie wir erzählen
... zu MEHR Wirksamkeit!

mit Schaubildern

ISBN 978-3-758-33126-8

Verdichten Sie Ihr Verständnis und bewegen sich selbstbewusst durch die Informationsfluten, die uns bedrohen, auseinander zu spülen!
Finden wir Klarheit in all unseren Gedanken, gefallen uns Herausforderungen und teilen wir gerne Erfolge. Denn gut unterhalten zu können, versichert uns immer guter Gesellschaft.

Mit diesem Sachbuch fällt es Ihnen fortan leicht, die Zeichnung im Kopf zu beginnen. Einfach erkennen: WAS WIR MACHEN!

Afsaneh
One from Many

ISBN 978-3-769-31572-1

Afsaneh is from Iran, the author from Germany. Is that enough for us to write a book?

Our dialogue grew from so many questions: about her homeland, life, and the future she seeks for her daughter.

- Beyond right and wrong, there is a place. We'll meet there. - knows Rumi. This invitation to dialogue became the foundation of a journey we took seriously - bridging cultures, histories, and perspectives.

Workbook: English
What was Iran?

ISBN 978-3-769-32048-0

This workbook accompanies *Afsaneh - One from Many* and encourages you to think beyond the question - What was Iran? - to reflect on: How do we want to live?

With engaging tasks, creative projects, and open discussions, it helps you understand the history and culture of Iran while sharpening your own perspective on the world. It connects the past, present, and future, inviting us to improve our vocabulary to find answers for living together harmoniously.

I would love to know what you discovered in the back rooms of your mind while reading this book.

Perhaps you'd like to leave us a review online? When readers become writers, it is yet another step toward engaging in dialogue.

And our cycle of *writing – reading – writing* finds its purpose!

Vera Ansén, born in 1972,
has been exploring narratives and media impact since 1992
—

always with the aim of overcoming speechlessness
and helping people amplify their causes.

We are all creators of culture, for we tell stories.

The realization that the head is round
so that thoughts can move freely
is key to the question:
How do we become MORE effective?

Stay curious — I certainly will.